WHEN
Spending
TAKES
THE PLACE OF
Feeling

KAREN O'CONNOR

THOMAS NELSON PUBLISHERS
NASHVILLE

Published in Nashville, Tennessee, by Thomas Nelson, Inc., and distributed in Canada by Lawson Falle, Ltd., Cambridge, Ontario.

The names, professions, ages, appearances, and other identifying details of the women whose stories are told in this book have been changed to protect their anonymity, unless they have granted permission to the author or publisher to do otherwise. All other identities are concealed as composites based on interviews and shared experiences.

Unless otherwise noted, Scripture quotations are from the NEW KING JAMES VERSION of the Bible. Copyright © 1979, 1980, 1982, Thomas Nelson, Inc., Publishers.

Scripture quotations noted NIV are from The Holy Bible: NEW INTERNATIONAL VERSION. Copyright © 1978 by the New York International Bible Society. Used by permission of Zondervan Bible Publishers.

Scripture quotations noted TLB are from *The Living Bible* (Wheaton, Illinois: Tyndale House Publishers, 1971) and are used by permission.

Library of Congress Cataloging in Publication Data

O'Connor, Karen, 1938–
    When spending takes the place of feeling / Karen O'Connor.
      p.   cm.
    Includes bibliographical references.
    ISBN 0-8407-3241-4
    1. Women—Finance, Personal. 2. Consumer credit. 3. Debt.
  I. Title.
  HG179.028 1992
  332.024'042—dc20   92-789
                                                                  CIP

Printed in the United States of America

1 2 3 4 5 6 7 - 97 96 95 94 93 92

To

Midge,
Rory,
Sherry,
Stephanie,
and
Suzanne
for loving and supporting me
just the way I am

Acknowledgments

I wish to thank the courageous women who stepped forward to share their experience, strength, and hope. This book would not have been possible without them. I also thank the many professionals who generously opened to me their writings, their research, their expertise, their observations on the topic of women and debt. I thank my agent Julie Castiglia, and the staff at Thomas Nelson Publishers for confirming my excitement and interest in this subject. And finally, I acknowledge and thank my husband Charles, for supporting me as a writer, as a woman, and as a Christian as we walk this path of recovery together with Jesus Christ.

Contents

Part Four: LIFE ON THE OTHER SIDE OF DEBT

A Personal Word from the Author

"Men and money are my higher power."

"As soon as I meet a man I stop earning."

"I pick men who can't even take care of themselves, yet I keep hoping they'll take care of me."

"I'm sixty-five years old. My mother and father are gone. My husband died. All my enablers are dead. It's up to me now, and I'm terrified."

"I love to spend money, but I don't know the first thing about earning it."

"I can't stop. I collect credit cards like a kid collects baseball cards. I have ten, and they're all maxed out."

Week after week I listened to Martha and Ginger, Jean, Louise, and other women share their experiences in various support groups, prosperity workshops, and Twelve Step recovery programs related to money issues.

Several of the women talked about their difficulties with male relationships in the area of money. Others shared the challenges they faced with credit card debt and overspending. Still others faced problems with earning, managing, and saving their money. Frequently, I heard the term *debtor*. I was uncomfortable with it.

I knew I had problems with men and money—but debting? I never considered myself a debtor. That label belonged to people who compulsively borrowed and overspent or gambled away their inheritances, or ran up their credit cards. I did none of these. On the other hand, my first husband was a debtor, and then I discovered my second husband had a related problem.

But it was only a matter of time until I discovered through one program—as members said I would if I kept coming back —just where I fit. I discovered that I was a debtor, all right. A self-debtor. One who continually gives away her money, her strength, her energy, her ideas, her very life to her mate, children, parents, and friends. It doesn't matter what she needs or how she feels about what they do to her. She needs their love, approval, and acceptance. She needs to be needed.

During the course of my recovery—which continues to this day—I learned about women and debt, about the compulsive disorder of debting, how closely it is tied to our feelings about ourselves as women, as wives and mothers, as friends and lovers. And I learned about how to recover one day at a time.

This book is a direct result of my experience in Twelve Step recovery programs, prosperity workshops, group therapy, individual Christian counseling, books—lots of books—and prayer—lots of that too.

Today I see women in debt all around me—women who on the one hand are strong, assertive, creative mothers, business professionals, artists, homemakers. But when it comes to money, many of them are, on the other hand, submissive, self-denying, fearful little girls depending on aging parents, on emotionally indifferent mates, or on irresponsible adult children.

When a woman puts other people's needs before her own, she is a woman in debt.

When a woman consistently earns less than she knows she is worth or than a comparable job pays, she is a woman in debt.

When she is terminally vague about what she earns, spends, saves or owes, she is a woman in debt.

When she stops earning or saving money the minute she gets involved in a relationship with a man, she is a woman in debt.

When she spends money on everyone—kids, spouse, friends, parents, neighbors, charities—but herself, she is a woman in debt.

When she compulsively buys things she neither wants nor needs, she is a woman in debt.

When time and again she overspends on food, clothing, trinkets, gifts, or vacations to alter her mood, she is a woman in debt.

Despite the extreme emotional and physical pain these behaviors create, the debting cycle continues until some women become so physically and emotionally ill they shut down altogether. Some end up on the street. Others contemplate or commit suicide rather than share their secret. And perhaps worst of all, most women remain in debt by simply living in our society, where debt is not only common, but acceptable—where one billion credit cards are in the hands of 100 million Americans.

In this book you will meet women in debt—overspenders, shopaholics, credit card abusers, gamblers, debting enablers, under-earners, self-debtors, and perpetual paupers.

My focus here is not on how to earn more and spend less, though you may discover how to do that as these women share their experiences, strength, and hope. Such matters are well-covered in other books, and I've listed some of them in the back under Supplementary Resources.

Instead my focus is on *debting as a compulsive disorder,* an emotional imbalance that keeps us from being, doing, and having all that we want and deserve.

It is my hope that you will discover, like the women in these pages, that the first step of recovery is recognition and admission. I found that labeling my disorder helped make it more real. Following that, I had the courage to take another step and then another one. The path to recovery is called *progress* not *perfection.*

"But I'm not a *compulsive* debtor," you may be saying right now. *Compulsive*—that's a pretty serious label. It can be a frightening one to those of us who have simply charged a bit too much this month or who bounced a couple of checks because we weren't paying attention to our balance.

On the other hand, compulsive debting by its very nature often gains a footing in our lives from just these "simple" but consistent and unconscious practices.

Irresponsible use of credit over time becomes credit card

abuse. Bouncing checks a few times a month soon escalates to a few times a week.

Helping out the man in our lives "till payday" one month can lead to *supporting* him the next. Covering for our adult children, when they blow their earnings on beer or drugs one month, can lead to bailing them out of jail the next. And in the process, we often deprive ourselves of the essentials we need to feel like whole people.

Cunning, baffling debt is as insidious as alcohol, cocaine, or heroin. We keep ourselves stuck on the merry-go-round of debt—many of us unable to stop it, others unwilling to get off because of the fear of taking total responsibility for our lives. And yet the day of reckoning comes to anyone who borrows from the present and steals from her future.

Although my own experience has provided the incentive for this book, I do not intend it to be an autobiography. My purpose here is to support you in recognizing where your weaknesses are with money, understanding their origins, and gaining tools for recovery and solvency.

To help you accomplish this I have divided the book into four parts. In Part One, I discuss what debt is—and isn't—and how and why women get into debt. You will quickly see, as those in recovery have, that financial debting is driven by emotional indebtedness—to ourselves. Women in debt spend rather than feel.

In Part Two you will meet women just like yourself—decent, loving, caring women—who have a problem with money. As they share their stories, I hope that you will draw on their experience and strength and use it to chart your own path.

Part Three is about recovery, facing the truth about yourself and sharing it with others. And Part Four is about life after debt. By the way, it does exist. And there is plenty of it, as you will see from the stories of women who are living there right now.

You will also discover, as have thousands of women before you, that recovery from debting is *not* really about money after all. It's about achieving spiritual, emotional, mental, and physical well-being. You will find—to your delight—that your most important creditor is *you,* and that as you become healed of the shame and self-abuse associated with debt, God can and will lead and direct you.

By bringing into balance your "inner account," you will be in a better position to attract the money, the job, and the relationships that will support you in being the person you want to be and having all the good God has for you—the good you desire and truly deserve.

I consider it a privilege to walk the path beside you!

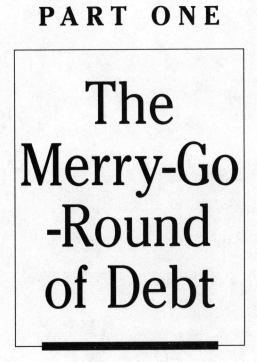

PART ONE

The
Merry-Go
-Round
of Debt

1

The Last Secret

A tall striking woman appeared in the doorway behind me at the weekly support group meeting. She paused for a moment, then found a place at the table directly across from me.

I had not seen her before. I assumed she was new. "I'm Audrey," she said in a loud whisper. The man next to her shook her hand and said, "Welcome."

I was drawn to Audrey from the moment I saw her. So were the men in the room! I guessed her to be about my age—fiftyish. She had style and grace, like a beautiful willow. I even admired the way she eased herself into the straight-backed chair. Her movements were as fluid as a summer breeze.

Her straight chestnut hair, drawn back and held in place by a print headband, exposed a beautiful face. Her full lips glistened with just the right shade of lipstick, and her cheeks were highlighted with a brush of red, the perfect touch beneath large, deep brown eyes.

The thin, gold chain around her neck, an array of slender bracelets on her left arm, and enormous hoop earrings set off the simple cream-colored silk blouse she wore. It all works, I thought to myself. Here's a lady who knows how to put herself together.

My mind wandered for a moment. A model. I bet she's a model for Nordstrom or Saks, I told myself. Then what's she doing here? At a meeting for people with money problems? She looks like she could buy and sell whatever she wanted. I hoped she'd tell her story.

As the hour went on and various people shared their experiences and feelings, I noticed Audrey's eyes mist on several occasions. She pulled out a handkerchief, dabbed the corners of her eyes, shifted nervously in her chair, and then folded and unfolded her hands on the table in front of her. The bright red polish on her impeccably manicured nails created a pleasing contrast to her fair skin.

Suddenly she was speaking. I couldn't wait to hear what she had to say. "I'm Audrey." She introduced herself, blinking back tears. "I'm in trouble with money. I feel like a child," she said softly. "I'm fifty-two years old, and I don't know a thing about it. I'm divorced. I have three grown children. I was married to a prominent corporate attorney in Great Neck, Long Island—that's in New York," she added, perhaps assuming Californians might not know the location.

"And I'm $30,000 in debt." She lowered her head, as a small girl might after making a true confession. "I don't know how it happened, actually. I just never had enough after the divorce. I was always behind. It was so easy to use my credit cards," she added. "The banks make them so appealing." A faint smile crossed her lips.

"My husband and I had been married for twenty-five years. We were comfortable, or so I thought. We had everything—the cars, the club, the clothes, a home in the city, and a summer place in Montauk.

"Then he met someone playing golf, and that was the beginning of the end. It was as if he had been waiting for an excuse to leave me."

Suddenly Audrey broke down. She sobbed, softly at first and then everyone in the room could hear her. I choked back my own tears. This was my story, almost word for word. It was about a different town and a different husband, but it was the same story.

She had been raised in a family much like my own. A solid Midwestern family with solid values. We went to church. We took family vacations. We entertained family and friends. We had a good, comfortable life. We even spent part of one summer on Montauk Point!

And then, like Audrey, I attended a small Christian college for women, graduated, married a law student, struggled through the bar exam with him, had three babies in five years, and woke up twenty years later divorced, alone, frightened, and overwhelmed with broken relationships, low self-esteem, and no sense of how to handle, spend, invest, or deal with money. I was a child in a forty-one-year-old body.

I wanted to put my arms around Audrey, give her a hug, and let her know we were all in this together. But that would come later. For now, I knew she needed to cry, to let out the pain and the grief and the shame—the terrible shame we feel as women when we're finally willing to admit that we are alone, scared, and penniless, that we fear ending up on the street or stuck in an extra room in the home of one of our adult children.

The shame of driving a twelve-year-old car when all our adult lives we've had a new car every two years. The pain of watching friends' marriages weather the storms of affairs and graduate school and sick kids and aging parents and knowing ours didn't make it.

Believing that somehow we weren't enough—not pretty enough, thin enough, sexy enough, patient enough. Enough, whatever that is, we weren't it. Deep in our guts we honestly believe that we're defective in some way that can never be fixed.

Audrey's soft voice startled me out of my thoughts. "I have seven charge cards," she said. "It's the only way I've been able to survive. I've never had a real career. I considered modeling when I was younger, but then I married, and the children came, and . . . well, you know the story," she said, looking around the room.

"I have almost nothing to show for the divorce. I netted about $100,000, but I went through that in three years. I tried to make wise decisions, talked to people, invested in some land. But it's gone, every penny is gone.

"I'm working at Nordstrom now. I moved to San Diego last year after my last son was married. I decided it was time for a change, time to think of myself, though I'm not very good at that.

"I worked at Macy's when I was in high school, so I guess selling women's clothing seemed like something I could do. I made $25,000 last year and I have $5,000 more than that in debt! A friend of mine figured out that at 20 percent annually I owe $500 a month in interest alone. That's exactly my share of the rent where I'm living."

DEBT TRAP

Audrey is not the only woman (or man) trapped by debt. Between 1950 and 1990 the average American's debt has increased from 10 percent of disposable income to between 20 and 25 percent.

For people with such high debt compared to their income and assets, bankruptcy often seems to be the only option. And many take that route. But those in Twelve Step recovery groups, such as Debtors Anonymous, Gamblers Anonymous, Overcomers Outreach (based on the model of Alcoholics Anonymous), and other solvency programs, have discovered that debting is an emotional disease—much like alcoholism, overeating, and drug abuse. It is a disease that never gets better, only worse, over time. Bankruptcy simply delays the inevitable, unless a person takes steps to recover.

Bankruptcy doesn't work because being in debt is not really a *money* issue. It is an issue of self-esteem and our feelings of not being enough, doing enough, or having enough. Women in debt try to fill the emptiness inside by spending money on themselves or others.

Audrey and I myself and every other woman in debt I know struggle with the same basic issue—low self-esteem. The emotional hole in each one of us is so big you could drive a truck through it. New clothes, a new car, or a new relationship won't fill it. Spurts of generous giving to others won't fill it either.

When these things don't work, many of us go to the other extreme. We become misers, hoarding our money, denying ourselves even basic clothing, nourishing food, adequate housing.

And when that doesn't work either, some women in debt—like Rhonda—consider suicide. "One year I was so despondent over my credit card bills I told myself that if I couldn't get a handle on them before the end of the year, I'd just end it. But then I found Debtors Anonymous and that was the turning point for me."

The steps to recovery are not set in stone. There are a number of paths. You may wish to map out your own plan based on what you read here. But the point is *women who surrender to God, then commit, plan, and take action, will get well.* It's that simple—and challenging. Recovery requires ruthless honesty and a relentless commitment to God and to ourselves—a course of action unfamiliar to most of us.

As women, we have learned our lessons well in this culture. The very traits that got us into trouble with money in the first place—self-denial, loyalty in the extreme, service, submission, cordiality—are often those admired as feminine and nurturing.

We are taught to be "other-centered," to rescue, take care of, and look after everyone except ourselves. And when the strain of living an other-centered life wears us down, we spend, gamble, hoard, or charge in a desperate attempt to give ourselves something, anything, to keep down the pain.

Like Audrey, you did not go into debt suddenly. Neither did I. The problem started years ago while we were growing up. How we got that way and what we can do about it is the subject of this book. But first I want to introduce another woman in debt, a woman quite different from Audrey and me—and a woman exactly the same in many ways.

The Clean Scene: Kathleen's Story

"I realize now I've always had a problem with money," said the petite brunette in her mid-thirties. "I guess you could call it my last secret. I'd rather talk about anything else—sex, my job, religion, my boyfriend, you name it. Anything but money. The whole subject of debt, credit cards, spending plans, and budgets terrifies me. I've never had enough money, and if I did I wouldn't know what to do with it anyway."

Kathleen's eyes filled up as she shared her story. "Last week it really hit me. I was standing on a ladder washing my apartment windows. All of a sudden I realized what I was doing. This was my fourth apartment in three years, and I'd scrubbed every one of them. I have a cleaning fetish," she added, laughing nervously. "It probably sounds ridiculous, but it's true.

"I believe it started the summer I turned ten. Until that year, we had lived on a small two-acre chicken farm in the Midwest. Then we lost everything. I'm still not sure how or why. It's one of those family secrets that no one talks about. Anyway, my dad was so devastated when the farm went under, he couldn't work for months. We moved to a small rented house in town. Then a friend of his offered him a part-time job washing windows and cleaning offices at night and on weekends. He continued that job till I was out of high school."

Kathleen pushed up the sleeves of her denim shirt, ran a hand through her short hair, and sighed deeply. "That particular summer I remember my father telling me I was old enough to help him wash windows. He said he could use a helper but didn't have enough money to hire someone, and he thought I'd be a great window washer. I felt very special standing beside him—he on one ladder and me on another. He even took me to the store with him to buy the supplies.

"After that whenever my dad had more work than he could do by himself, I got to help. In fact, those are the only times I remember spending any time with him." Kathleen laughed, sniffed back the tears, and nervously wiped her nose with the back of her hand.

"He didn't believe in socializing," she continued. " 'Waste of time,' he used to say. And he had a rule about money after we lost the farm. I'll never forget it. Money is for 'necessaries,' he said. And dancing lessons or pretty clothes or eating out definitely were not on his list of 'necessaries.'

"One of his most often-repeated statements was 'We don't have money for that.' Yet there had been plenty of money for paint and lumber and chicken feed when we lived on the farm —and for his cleaning supplies and his truck—important things that would last, he said. So my mother and I shopped garage sales and thrift stores for clothes. In my whole childhood I don't think I ever had an article of clothing that cost more than a dollar or two, and never ever something new."

Kathleen doodled on a piece of paper as she talked. "Cleaning, fixing things up—it's all I know. God, that's hard to face. As I stood on the ladder washing the windows it was like I was ten years old all over again. I wondered if my dad would approve. He's been dead for five years, but I've just gone right on washing windows, wanting him to be proud of me."

Her voice escalated for a moment, then mellowed. "I even got a thrill out of buying a new bucket and new blades and a can of paint. I raced through the hardware store like most women run through Penney's or Mervyn's. I put $200 worth of stuff on my Visa card in less than an hour. Necessaries," she said with a laugh. "All of it for the apartment—for the frigging apartment. It's not even mine. I don't own it. Who knows how long I'll live there. And yet I went into debt again, so I could *clean*. And I have never ever spent $200 on myself at one time. Never!"

Silence settled over the room like a blanket. Women around the table were beginning to see and hear themselves in Kathleen's story.

"Even my clothes are the same. These jeans are eight years old. Got 'em at a garage sale. Fifty cents! The same with shoes and shirts. I own two dresses. I got both of them at a thrift shop. I'm thirty-four years old, but I'm still living like that ten-year-old kid, terrified to spend money on myself, yet up to my ears in debt for 'necessaries'—like my truck. Can you believe that? I drive a truck, just like my dad did."

Audrey and Kathleen, like millions of other women, grew up in families where money was used to manipulate and control, to alter moods, to rescue, to reinforce certain kinds of behavior.

As adults, such women find themselves using money in the same destructive way, building debts by indulging themselves in things they neither need nor really want. Nor can they afford them.

Or they may find themselves in the opposite camp, terrified to spend money for fear of unleashing its power over them. Still others go into debt by rescuing someone else. They act on every hard-luck story they hear, financing a car for a teenage son, taking out a second mortgage on a home to help a boyfriend pay off his consumer debts, allowing a divorced friend to move in rent-free.

Before we can fully appreciate and understand the underpinnings of this compulsive behavior, however, I think it would be helpful to define the word *debt*.

WHAT IS DEBT?

Debt, pure and simple, is money or service owed to a creditor—a person or institution. In the world of finance, there are two kinds of debt, *secured* and *unsecured.*

To secure something is to make it safe. A secured loan is kept safe for the lender by means of *collateral*—an item of equal or greater value, which the lender holds during the repayment period. The pink slip on your car, for example, is collateral for your automobile loan. If you can't keep up your payments, the lender repossesses your car. You lose your car (and your credit rating), but you don't owe any more money. The lender does not lose money, because he now has your car, a good example of Proverbs 22:7, "the borrower is servant to the lender."

Any time you pledge a piece of property—a computer, a life insurance policy, jewelry, real estate, stock certificate—as collateral for a sum of money you borrow, you have entered into a secured loan—not secured for you, but for the lender. And you risk losing that security.

Technically you could say that a secured loan is not really a debt since the item or property of equal value keeps you accountable for repayment. But for women with compulsive behavior around money, even a secured loan can be a powerful and destructive tool.

On the surface, it may seem perfectly in order to purchase a car or a piece of office equipment on an installment plan. But as many women in debt have discovered, even a secured loan feeds into the cycle of debt they are trying to break. And in the event they cannot keep up the payments, the car or equipment is repossessed, fueling the self-hatred and helplessness that provoked going into debt in the first place. In my experience, a woman is better off paying cash or doing without until she has embarked on a disciplined program of recovery.

Unsecured loans are another matter. Groceries, clothing, cosmetics, restaurant dining, gas for your car, theater tickets, and other items you charge on your Mastercard, Visa, American Express, or Diner's Club accounts are not tied to collateral. Neither are spontaneous loans ($10 till payday, $10 for a pizza) made between family and friends.

Unsecured debt is where we get into the most trouble. We have bought the lie "Buy now. Pay later." And we do *pay* in more ways than one. Which brings up the other side of debt, the side that is not so simple or easily defined, or as readily acknowledged among women. It is the *emotional* side of debt, where we spend or borrow or loan money without regard for our well-being.

This behavior is usually compulsive, fueled by our unconscious need to keep the lid on our pain and fear and grief—known or unknown. We can't stop no matter how hard we try, no matter how much we know. Spending, in whatever form, takes the place of feeling.

THE MASK OF SELF-DEBT

Compulsive spending, when driven by the unconscious, leads to a more subtle form of debt—something called *self-debt*. Self-debt is also money or services owed to a creditor. The creditor, however, is *you*.

From my point of view, *all* debt, secured or unsecured, is self-debt. When we use goods and services without paying for them immediately, we not only take from the creditor, but we take from ourselves as well. Self-esteem, integrity, and personal responsibility fall as we depend on others to do for us what we can and should do for ourselves—pay as we go.

The reverse is also true. When we take from ourselves to do for others what they can and should do for themselves we go into self-debt.

When we rescue or help boyfriends, husbands, and adult children capable of earning, we rob them of the opportunity to work through their own problems, to discover their own resources. And in the process we steal from ourselves—money, time, energy, goods, or services that are necessary to our own survival and well-being.

GIVING TO GET

Does that mean we never give a gift, help a friend in desperate straits, or lend a hand to a struggling adult child? Of course not. It is one thing to offer honest assistance within the limits of time and available resources. It is quite another matter, however, to give in order to get—which is often the case with women in debt. Our motives are generally more intense than those of women who merely wish to buy a new car or provide a night or two of shelter for a friend in need.

Our motives often go back to childhood. We spend, borrow, or loan money in order to feel better about ourselves, to gain the attention, affection, and approval that we missed out on while growing up.

We help capable adult friends with mortgage and car payments. We turn over our gas cards to teenage children. We charge a new suit on our Visa card for our boyfriend or mate so he can interview for a job. We buy our parents hundred-dollar gifts when our budget or spending plan clearly prohibits such extravagance.

On the outside our motives may appear generous, even loving. On the inside, however, we know differently. Giving to, taking care of, and providing for others raises our self-esteem and alters our mood. We are actually giving in order to get. To get that good feeling, to get the approval and affection of someone else, to get out of an unpleasant mood.

I remember two months in a row when my husband and I received financial aid from the Deacon's Fund at our church in order to pay our rent. I was humiliated. I had always prided us on *giving* to the fund for the needy. I never anticipated being a recipient. That experience showed me how resistant I was to being vulnerable. I was much more comfortable, and in control, as the giver.

This experience also showed me an important difference between a woman who gives, "no strings attached," and the type of woman who gives in order to get something for herself. Those who give because they cannot risk being vulnerable are *compelled* to give. Compulsive giving creates a sense of power and authority. Such women must give. They don't have a choice.

Some of them believe unknowingly, as I did, that it is the *right* thing to do. Others don't even think about it to that extent. They do it quite simply, because at some level they *have* to.

They charge, loan, spend, borrow, give, take, hoard, lose, or gamble time and again. And then they wonder where all their money went, why there never seems to be enough, why *they* seemingly are never enough.

Debt—no matter how you define it or speak about it or use it—is real. Being in debt is a *serious* condition. It should never be taken lightly. It has the potential to destroy everyone and everything important to you—family, jobs, friends, your marriage, even your health, as millions of women in debt can attest.

Such women, by their own admission, use debt to manipulate their own and others' lives, to cover up their feelings, to punish or reward themselves, to help or hold hostage family and friends. To a woman in debt, any reason will do. You may be one of them. If you are, you may recognize in yourself some or all of the following characteristics that seem to be present in the lives of women in debt.

COMMON CHARACTERISTICS

A woman in debt is a long time in the making. The roots run deep.

1. Typically, you grew up in an emotionally distant home.

You did not see honest displays of anger, joy, sadness, love, or grief. Perhaps you were quieted down when you became excited, or you were told to "cool it," or to consider others, or not to make noise or show your temper. You may have been rewarded in some way for being the even-tempered one or the dependable child.

Beyond that, your perceptions of your own feelings may have been largely ignored or denied. "Don't tell me you're sad. There's nothing to be sad about." "If you complain one more time I'll give you something to be upset about—something you'll never forget."

If you told your mother that your brother hurt your feelings, she may have told you to "be a big girl" or not to "make a mountain out of a molehill." Parents or grandparents may have used some other time-worn clichés that, in summary, told you to stuff your feelings. They didn't count.

2. You controlled other people through spending.

You may have learned as a child to manipulate your parents or others through spending. A new dress, an ice cream cone, or the latest game or toy satisfied you for the moment. Over time, you saw how easy it was to get the attention you needed. Display strong feelings, and someone would spend money on you. It became a way of life.

3. You spend money in order to change your feelings.

You may be threatened by feelings of rage, jealousy, or anger. You "handle" them by treating yourself to something new —a quick trip through Target, a few necessities at the Price Club, a sweater on sale at The Rack, or a "must-have" at Saks, and within an hour or so you feel better, lighter, happier. Even if you don't have the cash to pay for these items, it's no problem. You can charge them. No need to worry today over what doesn't have to be paid for till next month.

4. You accept the message that you were not important enough to spend money on.

Like Kathleen, perhaps you discovered early that there wasn't enough money for you. Money was for important things like cars and furniture and rent or other members of your household. Someone in your family may have consistently reminded you that "money doesn't grow on trees" as if you thought it did! If you were a younger child in your family, you may have grown accustomed to wearing hand-me-down clothes, and if you longed for something brand-new just for you, you were led to feel guilty.

As an adult you cannot bring yourself to buy even the necessities. You make that pair of shoes work yet another season. You mend the blouse and patch the jeans. "They're good enough," you tell yourself. "Money doesn't grow on trees."

5. You equate spending with emotional fulfillment.

Every spring and fall you're the first one in line for the sales at the local department stores. You're not sure why, but you're always there. You remember your mother taking you shopping for school clothes and summer shorts and bathing suits. They were special times for you.

Shopping and lunch at a nice restaurant with your mother twice a year set the pattern in motion. You remember her smiling and admiring you in your new things. You returned home filled up inside and feeling pretty on the outside. Today you're looking for that same emotional fulfillment, even if you have to spend money to get it.

6. You associate spending with excitement.

Perhaps your father was a traveling salesman. He never knew where his next check was coming from. The entire family lived on the edge. When sales were up, there were new clothes, ice cream for dessert, and maybe a summer vacation. When sales were down, you watched your parents scrape their change together to put a meal on the table. You never knew what to expect, but one thing for sure—it was never dull at your house. Today you keep yourself broke, living from paycheck to paycheck, in order to keep the drama going, to feel "alive."

7. You fear the power of money so you chronically under-earn.

For many women in debt money appears to have a life of its own. If you allow yourself to have a penny more than you absolutely need, you fear losing control. To ensure your safety you take dead-end, no-stress jobs that keep you safe—and stuck. You wouldn't dream of owning a comfortable car, or wearing a silk blouse, or taking an art class, or enrolling in a graduate program, or signing up for a cruise. Those things are for people with money—people with power—people who like to flaunt their prosperity. Or so you've been told! Women who consistently and deliberately under-earn are terrified to give themselves permission to be creative, exciting, attractive, and intellectually stimulating. Nice girls should be seen and not heard.

8. You feel worthy only when you spend money on others.

If you grew up in a home where your mother was a full-time caregiver, then your sense of worth may be directly connected to how much you do for others and how little you do for yourself. You may be the kind of woman who would rather go into debt than cut down on gift-giving. You are the one to buy a bag of groceries for the needy family, write a check for a friend's car payment, or provide music lessons and birthday parties for your children or grandchildren, even if it means you go without needed clothing or necessary dental care. Spending money on other people makes you feel good about yourself. You *have* to do it.

9. You feel helpless and childlike around money issues.

Just thinking about money brings on a migraine. You've never had a head for figures. You hate numbers and columns and checkbooks. You can't be bothered with all this financial planning business. It's for the wizards of Wall Street, not you.

Anyway, you're sure things will work out. They always do. They'll never get totally out of control. And if they do, well there's bound to be someone to take care of you. You're a child at heart, carefree and innocent. You believe it's the way God made you. And you aim to stay that way, even if it costs you your life.

10. You live in a state of terminal vagueness.

Yes, you have a savings account, you think. You do keep track of your checks, but you round off the balance to make it easy. If you forget your check ledger you jot down the number and amount on a napkin and stuff it in your purse. You can enter it later. And on it goes. You have some notion about your financial picture, but it's fuzzy. You can't quite bring it into focus. You're terminally vague.

she said. "For the next year, I continued
would never ride again."

d of debt whirls us around and around.
ontinue the ride is a complex issue. For
uying on credit, the excitement of betting
power of buying expensive gifts keeps us
ther ride, then another and another until
what is good and right, healthy and appro-
e in this position because, as children, we
o look out for ourselves.

debt began the summer of 1960, a month
nd and I were married. We were living in a
om apartment in Southern California and
eeded for the time being—except a televi-

and we saw no reason to wait. We even
ve had this entertainment center at home
ney on movies and other outside amuse-

ash from wedding gifts to pay outright, but
to buy it "on time." I remember the thrill
irst piece of furniture together. We walked
e the one we wanted, and took it home. We
s intact, and we had only a small monthly
next year. It was so simple—so simple, in
ext twenty years of our marriage we were
debt.

HOW AND WHY

low do we get this way? And why? I doubt
s chooses—at least consciously—to be a
decision we make, like going to graduate
baby, or joining a church. That's why it's
baffling to most of us. We just know we're
nt to change it.

anting to change our behavior, however, is
d naive about the process. I think it's im-
ze the fact that we didn't get into debt over-
t get out of it overnight. The road to recov-

11. You're addicted to money, whether you spend or hoard.

You don't touch alcohol. You never overeat. But your substance of choice is money. You either spend it as fast as you
get it or stash it away to the point of insanity, depriving yourself of even basic human needs. Everything in your life revolves around how much money is involved. If a friend invites
you to a movie and lunch, your first thought is "How much is
it going to cost me?" If you see an ad for a weekend car camp
in the desert, you look at the cost first, your need for a break,
second. If someone gives you a gift of money for your birthday
or other occasion, you put it in the bank immediately. You
never even consider spending it as it was intended—on a gift
for yourself.

12. You have little sense of your worth as a person.

You are an expert on what other people need and want and
deserve, but you have no idea what is good for you. You never
stop long enough to find out. This lack of insight keeps you
from making wise and healthy choices for your own well-
being. But you haven't known that because you don't know
your worth as a person, as a woman, as a child of God.

Instead of expressing your feelings and allowing them to
help you make important decisions, you stand on the side-
lines wringing your hands. So out of touch are you with your
own needs and wishes, you continually fret over money and
puzzle over such basic decisions as what to buy, what to
wear, what to eat, where to go, even what to think.

In the following pages, women like you share their stories
about their relationship with debt—stories that can help you
see and understand more clearly your particular patterns
around money.

Many of the stories have happy endings, or beginnings, depending on your point of view. These women are in recovery
programs where they are dealing with the emotional issues
that have for too long fueled their unhealthy relationship with
money.

My hope is that their courage and their testimonies will cause you to take action in your life. Recovery, as you will see and experience, is available to any woman in debt who claims it. The first, and most important, step is being willing.

for the payments,"
paying off the bike

The merry-go-rou
How and why we
some the magic of
on the lottery, or th
coming back for an
we lose all sense of
priate. Many of us a
were never taught

My own ride with
after my first husba
furnished one-bedr
had everything we
sion set.

We wanted one,
rationalized that if
we'd spend less m
ments.

We had enough
we decided instead
of purchasing this
into the store, cho
still had our saving
payment over the
fact, that for the
never again out of

What happens?
that any one of
debtor. It's not a
school, or having
so insidious and s
in debt, and we w

The danger in v
being impatient a
portant to recogni
night, and we wor

Ho
Won

Linda, a wi
debt for as
how or why. She's
Her parents borrow
ition to a tractor fo
and she's continue
break now that she'

Esther said her h
and discipline. "We
proudly throughout
from anybody. If we
remembers, at age s
one. But in a family
for such things. And
could have earned th
that only her brothe

"I vowed then that
didn't care what it w
own, I bought that
credit. Ironically, som
that was the end of th

ery—like any road—has restaurants and markets, shopping malls and car dealerships. We cannot stop using money in the same way a recovering alcoholic can stop drinking or an addict can stop using drugs. We must spend money, even as we recover from abusing it.

But we can pay attention to *how* we get into debt so we can gain some understanding of *why*. It usually starts with the little things.

Borrowing small amounts from family and friends

"I never carry cash," says thirty-one-year-old Rita. "I know if I have it I'll spend it. But I guess that doesn't make sense because I end up borrowing from friends and then spending their money—for coffee and lunch or a movie. I've lost a lot of friends that way. I always plan to pay them back, and sometimes I do. But I never seem to get caught up. I always owe somebody something, and half the time I don't remember how much or who I owe it to."

Bouncing checks

Leslie says she's in the habit of bouncing checks. She's not a thief. She's just an underpaid, overworked county social worker who says she rewards herself at the end of a hard case with something pretty, something nice, something clearly not in her budget. "I keep telling myself I'm going to wait till I know I have enough in the bank, but then I see a dress or a piece of jewelry or a book, and I just have to have it. For the last few years I feel like I've spent most of my free time dodging calls from the bank and closing and starting new accounts."

Kiting checks

Janet, on the other hand, writes checks for more than she has in her account—especially the week before payday. She cashes a check at the supermarket on Friday night and hopes it won't clear before she can deposit her paycheck the following Monday after work. *Kiting* is the name of this game, one we all play from time to time and get away with. But it's a form of debt, nonetheless.

Buying things we don't need or want

Renee said her debts involve things she doesn't need or even want. "I have a Cuisinart™ food processor I never use because I hate to cook. I have a gold Cross™ pen and pencil set that I've never taken out of the box. And I even have a gorgeous piece of Samsonite™ luggage; yet I don't travel. I can't tell you what all this means. I vaguely remember thinking that if I have the right equipment, maybe I'll feel more like cooking, or writing letters, or taking a trip. It's nuts," she said with a wave of her hand.

"Actually, I'm beginning to make some sense of it now that I'm in therapy. My mother always had a lot of stuff around the house she never used. I remember a sewing machine that sat in the corner of our dining room for years. She didn't sew, and I never once saw it open. When I asked her if she was going to start making clothes for my sister and me, she said, 'I just might do that one day. I just might do that.' And that was the last time we ever talked about it.

"Another time my brother and I snooped in her closet to see what she got us for Christmas, and I saw this gorgeous red wool coat with a tag on it and a beautiful hat with fur trim. I had never seen her wear either one. I couldn't ask her about them because then she'd know we were in her closet. But I wondered about that coat and hat for a long time afterward. Then the thoughts just faded away until I began talking to my therapist about my childhood." Renee took a deep breath and looked out the window.

"Maybe someday I'll have the courage to ask my mother about it. But then I'd have to admit that I looked in her closet," she said with a childlike giggle. "I wonder if she'd be mad at me after all these years."

Shopping to make us feel better

Annette says playfully that she was born to shop. "Something special happens in a mall," she says. "It's magic. The colors and the fabrics, and the sounds, and the windows. I've always been hooked on clothes, ever since my dad started calling me his "pretty little lady." I guess in a way I still dress for him. But I'm thirty-four, and he's not picking up the bills like he did when I was a kid. I spent nearly $8,000 on clothes this year, and I only make $30,000."

Wanting things we cannot afford and buying them anyway

"I had worked for six years straight without a vacation," said Dana, with a note of self-pity in her voice. "As far as I was concerned I deserved that cruise," she said, talking about a recent ten-day trip to the Bahamas. "I'll probably be paying for it for the next five years, but it was worth it."

Lucy, who lives in Oregon, said she bought a new, larger car when her parents, sister, and brother-in-law made plans to visit her one year for the Christmas holidays. "I knew I couldn't get everyone into my little VW so I bought a new four-door Honda," she said. "All I was doing was spending money—trying to make a nest for myself. I bought a set of china for six, placemats, napkins, the whole deal. And I spent $100 on tree ornaments. I wanted desperately for my family to see that I was doing well."

Lucy said she never told them that she had to take out a huge loan to cover all these expenditures. "It was ridiculous when I look back now," she said. "They could have rented a car for the few days they were here, and we could have used the plastic dishes I had on hand. I haven't used the china or the napkins since their visit four years ago. And a small tree with some colored lights and balls would have been sufficient. I'm still paying for that spending spree—in more ways than one."

Putting other people's financial needs ahead of your own

Betty, a sixty-five-year-old widow, by her own admission, is a perfect example of this behavior. When her husband died, he left her a house that was paid for and a $500,000 life insurance policy. "That was five years ago," she said wistfully, "and most of my assets are gone—except the house. And I'll lose that if I don't get a handle on this spending. As you can see," she said, pointing to her clothes, "I'm not exactly ready for the Saks runway. I haven't bought myself a new piece of clothing in years. Actually, I don't need anything.

"My kids are my downfall. They're all struggling with mortgage payments and orthodontia for my grandkids and car repairs—and well, you know what it's like. We've all been through it. I can't stand watching them suffer through these lean years. I bought my one son a car, and I gave my daughter and her husband the down payment on a condo and on and on it goes. I'm an absolute sucker when it comes to my kids. I figure I can do without, but they shouldn't have to. Course they don't have a clue that I've gone through this much money so fast. My son would kill me if he knew. That's why I've got to get some help—before it's too late."

Gambling to relieve stress

Joan likes to play a game of cards once in a while—for money—or bet on a race at the Del Mar track or buy a lottery ticket. At least that's the way it started. Now she says all she can think about is the next bet. "There's something about picking those numbers, or choosing a horse, or going for the winning hand. I can't explain it. It makes me feel good, alive, excited again." But Joan doesn't go to the track or the card room or the lottery window occasionally or just for fun anymore. Betting and gambling have become almost a business with her. She says she needs help.

DEBT AND DEPENDENCE

Observing our habits and practices with money is important. It's a good first step, but our search can't stop there. What we're really after is the *system of beliefs that supports the unwanted behavior.*

I began to see the truth about my own belief system one Saturday about two years ago while attending a life-changing seminar, titled "Prosperity, Success, and Codependence," offered by Christian counselor and psychologist Sondra Mehlhop.[1]

When I first read the flier for the workshop, I was attracted by the combination of words in the title, and how they were related. I had not yet made a connection between money and codependence in my own life, although I had attended several career and prosperity workshops, read books, and listened to tapes on the subject during the early 1980s. I remember hearing seminar leaders, preachers, authors, and other professionals talk about my right to the abundant life and God's will for me to have all my needs met—as well as the desires of my heart.

It *sounded* wonderful, but the minute I would put down the book or tape, or walk out of the meeting, I felt defeated. Prosperity and abundance were for other people—not for me. I was a classic example of what Christian author and talk show host Rich Buhler calls "the doctrine of eligibility."[2] I did not feel eligible or worthy. In fact, I couldn't even *imagine* it.

A month later, while sitting in Mehlhop's workshop, I realized that my real issue was not money at all but codependence—a term and concept that was just beginning to be talked about in recovery circles.

By my own definition and experience, I see a codependent as *a person who depends on a person who depends on and abuses a substance or activity to avoid reality.* In this case, the substance was money, and the activity was debting.

While I did not have any personal debt at the time, I suddenly realized that I had been *living* the reality of other people's debt for more than twenty-five years. Debt was a way of life for my first husband and me, and my second husband came into our marriage also rooted in debt.

Depending on men who depended on money was all I knew. I had enabled my first husband to keep us on the edge financially because I didn't know how to separate my identity from his. And I was doing the same thing in my second marriage. Once again I was depending on a man who depended on money—through debt. And I was beginning to experience hatred and rage against someone I loved deeply.

But where did this come from? My father was successful in business, and our family always seemed to have whatever we needed and most of the things we wanted. I couldn't find the root, yet I definitely had a problem with money.

As I was to discover that day, my conflict was actually tied to something much deeper. It was rooted in the five core symptoms of dysfunction, which Pia Mellody outlines in her classic book *Facing Codependence[3]: difficulty with self-esteem, with setting functional boundaries, with knowing our own reality, with acknowledging and meeting our needs and wants, and with expressing our reality moderately.*

Dr. Mehlhop organized her workshop around these five core symptoms as they relate to dysfunction with money. While talking with her during the course of writing this book, I was reminded again of her enormous warmth and kindness. Tall, graceful, and soft-spoken, Mehlhop obviously cares very much about women and their issues. As she spoke, she returned to Pia Mellody's model. Most of the women I spoke with, and those in the workshop, could strongly identify with these core symptoms.

Difficulty with self-esteem

Our first experience with self-esteem comes from our primary caregivers, usually our parents. In a functional home where the parents' self-esteem is intact, a baby girl can look into her mother's eyes and feel valued and loved. But a mother who has never known her own worth cannot mirror healthy emotions for her daughter. And so the girl begins to see her worth based on her mother's expectations and point of view. And depending on the emotional state of the parent, that worth can change from day to day.

For example, "money may be the only consistent symbol of love for a child as she grows up," says Mehlhop.[4] "If there is money spent in place of time and attention, then that individual learns to equate love with money." If money is withheld, especially for basic care such as food or hygiene or clothing, or if the child is ignored emotionally, then she grows up feeling unlovable.

She is likely to feel that if her parents don't provide even the necessities, then she can't be worth much. And if her family does not communicate about this and other important issues, the child is left to figure things out for herself, based on how she has been treated or mistreated.

A girl with healthy self-esteem, on the other hand, can feel valuable regardless of whether her mother sews her clothes or buys them, whether her parents drive a new car or an older one, whether she goes on a cruise or camps in the desert.

That same person as an adult still thinks well of herself regardless of her husband's position, her own desire to work or remain at home, or her children's performance at school or on the swim team.

A woman with low self-esteem, however, and what Pia Mellody calls "other-esteem" measures her value by what others think of her and how they view her performance—from the home she lives in to the clothes she wears.

For example, if the husband of a woman with low self-esteem is out of work she may internalize his situation, make it hers, and feel less than a whole person because of what he does or does not do. If her teenage son fails chemistry, she may feel it is a personal attack on her mothering process, and the old childhood feelings of "less than" surface again.

Mehlhop helps women with these shaming messages to look at the habits and patterns in their birth family. "I have them do a money tree," she said, "to see what the family occupations and attitudes are around money. This is very important work because it helps them see how their own attitudes and behavior have been shaped by one generation after another." We are not raised in a vacuum. Even the most neglected person is receiving messages that form the basis for her thoughts, feelings, and behavior throughout her life.

I remember my high school senior English teacher in a Catholic school telling me that I couldn't trust my feelings. "They will pave the way to hell," she said. I have never forgotten it. I was already a victim of low self-esteem, and that remark intensified my fragile viewpoint. I came to a point of thinking that if I invested *any* amount of time in myself, however small, I was being selfish.

As I look back now, I realize that my entire childhood at home and in Catholic schools was other-centered. I learned early to put my own needs aside and give to others. But those long-ago lessons excluded a component that I now see as essential: *Take care of yourself first—then give to others from your abundance.*

But I didn't learn that for forty years. As a result, I felt like a nomad in a desert most of my life. I had no boundaries, no clear way to shield myself from the unhealthy and unreasonable demands of others. And little or no joy.

Difficulty with setting functional boundaries

Women with low self-esteem need permission to create and exercise personal boundaries, to erect a kind of "fence" that allows us to protect our personal space, both externally and internally, and to be sensitive to the boundaries of others. We let people know our boundaries, and we discover theirs through language and movement.

For example, one day while walking into a supermarket a panhandler asked my husband for $10. Charles felt immediately intruded upon. The stranger didn't approach him sensitively. He simply pushed on Charles's boundary. And my husband pushed back by saying no in a firm voice.

By contrast, when the father of a friend of mine agreed to loan her a sum of money, using a piece of jewelry as collateral, they drew up a mutually acceptable repayment plan. This was an example of two people respecting each other's boundaries. He met her financial need. She met his need, and hers, for a payment schedule that they both could live with.

We are not born with boundaries. As babies, we are completely dependent. It is up to our caregivers to teach us how to form our boundaries and how to respond to those of other people. Women who have grown up in a home with dysfunctional practices around money generally have damaged, partial, or no boundaries at all regarding finances.

For example, if money was an issue of shame in your family —either not having enough or having too much and being embarrassed by it—then as an adult you may have no boundaries regarding money. You become an easy mark, one who writes checks freely, feels responsible for everyone's financial crises, and guilty if you spend on yourself when someone else is left wanting, regardless of how that person may have gotten that way.

If you received mixed messages at home where one parent gave away money and possessions without any thought for the well-being of the immediate family and the other parent hoarded what little he or she could salvage, then you may have partial or damaged boundaries—never clear about the right thing to do. This can be terrifying to an adult woman who has already been primed by our culture to take less than she deserves, whether at work or at home.

us has our own "reality." If we grew up in a dysfunctional me, however, we do not know what that reality is. We have ouble assessing our physical appearance and bodily needs nd distinguishing our feelings and thoughts from those of our arents or other significant authority figures. These conflicts how in our behavior.

Women who have a distorted reality about their appearance or bodily functions frequently deny themselves new shoes when the old ones are clearly worn out, avoid going to the dentist until they have an abscessed tooth or gum disease, or buy clothing only at thrift shops and bargain basements.

Many of us act out our emotions instead of verbalizing them. We may rage at people without cause, or pout or scream when we don't get our way, or shrink from any form of communication by simply leaving the scene.

Other women lose touch with their intellectual reality about money through conscious or subconscious parental messages, such as "Nice girls don't take money seriously"; "Women are born to shop"; "Leave money-making to the boys"; "Money is the root of all evil"; or the opposite directives that deify money: "You can't have too much of a good thing"; "The job's not important, it's what you make that counts"; "Hard work and honest pay are all that matter."

I don't recall hearing any of these messages during my childhood, but I do remember my mother encouraging me to get my teaching credential so I'd "have something to fall back on." I think the message there was "Be prepared in case of emergency." The emphasis was on earning as a last resort, not as a first choice.

Just as some young women are forbidden to work or are discouraged from pursuing a career, others may be driven out to the workplace before they are ready or are made to pay for items that are the responsibility of the caregivers. Still others may be denied the opportunity to explore the world of work and earning because it brings a sense of shame or inadequacy to the family.

I remember wanting to baby-sit when I was about twelve, ut my parents needed me to sit for my younger brother and ister. To me that wasn't the same. They didn't pay me for the b. I wanted to earn money from what I considered to be a *al* baby-sitting job.

I began to see that day what an unshakable founda   of
been laid down in my life for giving and enabling. My   he
are the most generous people I've ever known—alway.   tr
to help family and friends and the church financiall   a
they've been blessed for their giving. But the part I miss   p
didn't hear was that this kind of giving must *follow,* no   s
cede, meeting my own needs and the needs of my imme
family. I grew up without being taught how to create f
tional, personal boundaries, and like many women in de
nearly died trying to be all things to all people.

"The root of these mixed messages is toxic shame," sa
Mehlhop. "Shame that was poured into us as children—sham
that says that we are less than, less able, less capable, sham
that says we don't spend it right, earn enough, handle it cor-
rectly. Shame that is not ours. The fear of not being able to
survive financially without someone to take care of us is indi-
rectly tied to the fear of not being a complete person alone—
another example of dysfunctional or non-existent boundaries."

Our job in recovery, according to Mehlhop, is to "find the
messages that little girl received about money and self-worth,
then bring the functioning adult on board to reparent and
change those negative tapes."

This can be a long-term process, but an exciting one, as a
woman begins to take seriously, perhaps for the first time, the
spiritual and emotional resources that are already within her.
Some women find that working on these issues with a skilled
counselor who specializes in codependence can be very helpful.

Difficulty with knowing our own reality

Women who have problems setting boundaries usually have
difficulty experiencing what is true and real for them as well.
In fact, that is part of what makes it so difficult to set bound
aries. They often do not know where one person ends ar
they begin. They become easily enmeshed in other peopl
ideas, beliefs, preferences, and emotions.

But a woman's reality is a precious thing. It is her uni
perspective or point of view about life as she experienc   j
through her spirit, body, mind, emotions, and behavior.   r

My friend Marlene, on the other hand, came from a broken family and *had* to work to help with groceries and rent. So her reality was also denied. She was earning money for things that were her parents' responsibility to provide.

I have not seen Marlene in years, but I suspect she may have difficulty today spending money on things other than necessities, just as I've had a struggle believing that I could work and earn enough *for* necessities.

"The dysfunctional system," says Mehlhop, "claims that appearances are more important than reality." These and other parental tapes shape a young girl's view of life before she's had an opportunity to experiment and formulate what's right and true for her.

Difficulty with acknowledging and meeting our needs and wants

Mehlhop says much of her work is with clients who experience shame around money. "Especially having to do with *wants*. Many women can actually pay for what they *need* without feeling any shame, but have real trouble spending money for their wants." Some cannot even express their desire for a new car or a trip or a bouquet of fresh flowers without apologizing for it.

I've been a victim of this limited thinking and catch myself in the same mode even now, after years of recovery. I speak in terms of needs even when I purchase something that is more of a want. For example, if I shop for clothes, I buy only what I perceive as a need—a black shirt to go with last year's wool pants, a book that I need for a research project, a weekend trip that I can combine with an interview for an article I want to write, and so on. I find myself sneaking in my wants by calling them needs! I think that's a step in the right direction, but I notice how tied I am to the old way of seeing things.

My mother talks the same way. She's a beautiful dresser, but whenever I comment on a new outfit or a lovely accessory, she's quick to say, "It's your father. He insisted I buy this coat." Or she'll say with a roll of her eyes, "You know your father . . . if it was up to me, I'd. . . ." She might also remind me of how prudent she is. "You know I don't spend deprived that she cannot even bring herself to spend money on basic self-care. "It's one thing to feel shame around spending money on our wants," said Dr. Mehlhop, "but at a deeper level of dysfunction is shame over spending money on our needs—even in situations where the individual can afford it."

Gretchen, for example, has not had a pap smear or a breast exam or a dental check-up in ten years. She dismisses any reference to routine health care as expensive and self-indulgent. After a few minutes of conversation, she shared that her mother lived to be seventy-five and never went to a doctor. She had told Gretchen that women who "fawned over their bodies were stuck-up and selfish." Today, Gretchen, a woman of fifty-five years of age, actually believes that spending money on basic health care means preoccupation with oneself. Her mother's reality has become her own.

"The person who denies herself in this way," says Dr. Mehlhop, "is living as if she were a pauper—much like the woman we read about from time to time in the newspaper—a person who dies and leaves $100,000 under a mattress. For all practicality, she was living as a pauper. This is sometimes called 'money paranoia' or fear of not having enough. She hoarded or held onto her money and yet her lifestyle was one of a pauper."

Examples of this behavior are evidence that prosperity is a state of mind. "One can have money and be poor and one can also be prosperous without money. When we hoard money or use it to buy recognition, power, or affection," said Mehlhop, "then money has the power over our lives."

Before we can be responsible for appropriate self-care, we have to accept that we are equal to other people—not less than and not better than. That means that we have the right to meet our basic financial needs for food, clothing, and shelter before we give to others.

Self-care in terms of money is being willing to recognize that "we each have the right to enjoy our prosperity, and we have the right to decide how we're going to manage it," says Mehlhop. "A self-care boundary with money might be expressed in this way: 'I have the right to my own money, since I earned it or it has come to me in some way. I also have the right to decide how I will or will not spend it, to whom I will or will not give it, and what I will require in return.'"

Codependent women, however, struggle with this self-care boundary. "The dysfunctional behavior kicks in," said Mehlhop, "and they feel toxic or unhealthy shame over having more than someone else—even if the other person did nothing to acquire his or her own prosperity."

In order to care for ourselves in a healthy way, Mehlhop suggests, "money counseling may be necessary to determine one's financial needs realistically, and to create a plan that will include some money for wants, as well. I advise all my clients to get into group therapy or some kind of Twelve Step support program." These may include Debtors Anonymous, Overcomers Outreach, Al-Anon family groups, or CODA (Codependents Anonymous)—all modeled after the original support program of Alcoholics Anonymous. (See Supplementary Resources at the back of the book for further information.)

Mehlhop says that of all the books she's read on the topic of money, her favorite is *Money, Sex, and Power* by Christian author Richard Foster. "He proposes that we earn all we can so we can take care of self and family first, then save, spend, and give away all we can. If we do that, then money does not become an end in itself. To Foster that is a full life."

Dr. Mehlhop says she is beginning to see the value of this philosophy in her own life as well as those of her clients, especially her Christian clients, who believe that "ultimately money is not theirs, but rather, another of the many blessings from God."

Perhaps that recognition and acceptance is the most important realization we can have as we step down from the merry-go-round of debt and look at the healing God has for us. But before we look at recovery, I'd like you to meet some of the many women in debt who have agreed to share their experience, strength, and hope.

PART TWO

Women in Debt: Who Are We?

3

Overspenders

The topic of compulsive spending has interested Sharene Garaman[1] for over a decade. It is the focus of her doctoral dissertation in clinical psychology and a specialty in her therapy practice. Originally from Wyoming, she is now living and conducting her research in Southern California.

As we sat in her living room overlooking a beautiful outdoor assembly of plants and trees, Garaman, dressed in jeans and a smart-looking lime green shirt, talked about her commitment to learning all she can about the process of compulsive spending.

People have told her that she is one of the few professionals they've met who really understands the problem. "Little wonder," she said laughing. "I began researching this subject initially for myself—I was a compulsive spender—and then because of my friends. I saw many of them doing with money what I had done." But in the professional literature she read, Garaman found "very little on spending," unlike the large volume available on drug and alcohol abuse.

Because of this, Garaman is interested in arriving at a clear definition of overspending. "We don't yet know how to define this behavior," she said. "But we need a place to start." Garaman hopes to provide that starting place by the time she completes her doctoral thesis. "Some women, for example, believe that if they have an unlimited amount of money to spend and they're not in debt, then they're not compulsive spenders. But I think that's totally erroneous." There is more to the spending problem than simply being in debt.

HELP WITH BEHAVIOR

Garaman favors a behavioral approach to treatment—"partly because of what worked for me, what works for my clients, and as a result of what I was reading in my research. As a therapist I need to be able to tell my clients this is what I think and why, and this is what I do in this area," said Garaman. "Then a woman can decide whether or not she wants to work with me. But if the entire subject is vague, you can't make any headway. I need to be able to help people change their behavior."

For example, if a client says she can't handle her money and is overspending regularly, Garaman feels it is important to help the client "put the brakes on her behavior"—not simply look at her reasons for spending. "The emotional issues are important, but that can come later in the recovery process. Down the road the woman will learn what her spending habits mean about her, but meanwhile she continues to spend, and probably will spend even more money because therapy itself is anxiety-producing."

Garaman may ask her client to write down everything she spends money on. In her own life, she claims that listing her purchases was the single "most important recovery tool" she used. That may not be true for everyone, but it was for her. She said she did not need a long-term emotional catharsis to discover the how and the why. She just needed to see the evidence. "I was so appalled when I found out that I was spending 25 percent of my earnings on clothes that I stopped it right then. There was no getting around it. I just quit. Granted, I had to be at a point in my life where I could do that sort of thing," she added.

CONSPICUOUS CONSUMPTION

Garaman also feels that therapy and group recovery programs sometimes focus on the personal and emotional levels to the exclusion of the social and cultural influences. "We live in a very consumer-oriented society," she said, "and when you're defining compulsive spending, you have to take the culture into consideration. Not to do so would be incomplete.

"I come from Wyoming where spending is not as glamorized as it is here. I've never seen such conspicuous consumption anywhere as I have in Southern California. It gets to the point of vulgarity. When you're raised in this culture, I don't think spending is questioned to the degree it should be."

For example, "I was not a compulsive spender waiting to happen. My spending was precipitated by the culture. When I was eighteen I went away to school and worked part-time at Joseph Magnin," a department store equivalent to I. Magnin. "Most of the clerks I knew spent a good deal of money in that store. They had credit cards—always maxed out—and it was accepted behavior."

She stopped for a moment, then continued emphasizing her words. "I feel that's an important point," she added. "These people were older than me. They were my reference group— the ones I looked up to. If they did it, I thought I'd do it too. In addition, there was pressure to look good."

Garaman paused, reflecting on that experience. "So did I have a lot of emotional needs that needed to be filled? Yes. But was that the reason why I spent my money? Initially, I think not."

That early experience has had a great impact on the direction of her research and her work with clients. "In treating women with spending problems I feel it would be jumping the gun to focus on the emotional issues alone."

QUESTIONING THE CULTURE

Exploring the cultural influences may also involve looking at a woman's spiritual issues. For example, she may help such women rethink their goals for their lives by exploring the answers to a number of questions: "Is this the way you want to live your life? Do you want to spend this much energy acquiring objects? Do you really need the latest everything? Is this a worthwhile lifestyle?"

Women who have unlimited resources are more difficult to reach because they don't think spending is an issue. "But," says Garaman, "I think they're in just as much trouble as those with a finite amount of money who get into debt because of their spending. Maybe more so. Those who can't pay their bills are likely to wake up to their problem" and do something about it.

"Part of the recovery process is to get women who overspend to step back and question their values and the culture's values around this kind of excessive spending," she added.

"A lot of people still don't know that, however, because it hasn't been defined. In fact, from my research into American and British literature, I'm convinced that in this country we are at a stage of infancy when it comes to defining and understanding addictions."

She pointed to the ongoing debate over alcoholism as a disease. "If researchers cannot even agree on a definition of the alcoholic, after all that has been studied on this topic, then how can we expect to define a compulsive spender when there is so little research available?"

NOT ALL ADDICTS LOOK ALIKE!

Some professionals believe that addiction is addiction, regardless of its expression. If you have deep-seated, unresolved emotional issues, then you are prone to addictive behavior—whether overspending, overeating, overworking, or drug or alcohol abuse. Garaman says she resists this simplistic viewpoint. She sees it as unjust to lump all addictions together and to view all abusers as the same type of person.

She says it is valid, however, and can be helpful, to note some of the common characteristics of people who chronically overspend. In her experience these include:

Magical thinking

They seem to believe that the money they need will come from somewhere.

Projecting the good girl image

Spenders aren't stopped for spending, the way alcoholics may be stopped for drinking. "Let's face it! A woman is not going to get pulled over to the side of the road for having too many Nordstrom sacks in her car!" said Garaman.

Dressing well and being socially aware

Some of these women wear gold jewelry, full make-up, and the most fashionable clothes even to an aerobics class!

Being concerned with how they are received by others

It is important to them to look good and to be well thought of. One woman said she dressed to impress others and was aware that she did.

Spending on others

Some women justify their overspending as valid because they see it as selfless. They don't deserve nice things—but others do—so they spend for family and friends and employees. They are usually the ones who always find the "perfect" gift, regardless of the cost.

Wavering self-esteem

Generally women with low self-esteem use spending as a way to feel better about themselves.

Some of these characteristics may also be true of people with other addictions, according to Garaman. Therefore, one of her primary goals is to distinguish more precisely the compulsive spender from people with other behavioral disorders.

Garaman also sees a distinction between compulsive shoppers and compulsive spenders. For example, she said, "There are some women who wander the malls to the exclusion of other responsibilities, spending an inordinate amount of time shopping, whether or not they actually go into debt. The point here is that they use shopping as a way to avoid responsibilities.

"Then there are women who overspend but don't like to shop. They go into a store, spend their money, and leave. And of course, there are those who shop and spend—a lot of money and a lot of time." Garaman again referred to the importance of defining these behaviors.

DISTINGUISHING WANTS FROM NEEDS

Frequently women get into debt because they cannot distinguish their wants from their needs. One woman said she now sees that God has provided enough money for all her needs, but she keeps spending it on her wants! This is probably true of most of us. But distinguishing our needs from our wants can be a problem. Many overspenders don't know the difference.

For example, "I went shopping with one of my best friends, who is a cruise director," said Garaman. "She wanted to buy a new evening gown. She had recently lost weight and was eager to buy something that looked good on her. There were about four dresses she liked at $300 to $400 apiece."

Garaman said she shared with her friend one of her own realizations. "We can't buy everything we look good in. But that was something of a revelation to my friend," she added. "She wanted all of them.

"I suggested she buy just one because she didn't really need four. I wanted to help her interrupt her overspending process. That day she bought just one. But the next day she sent someone from the ship to pick up the rest of the dresses.

"At that point she really believed that she *needed* all of them. Intellectually she knew differently, but emotionally, she was sure she needed them."

Another woman Garaman worked with had many clothes but was so overwhelmed by them, she ran around in jeans and a T-shirt because she couldn't make a decision about what to wear.

Garaman has dealt with many women, like her friend, who struggle with the difference between a want and a need. "Actually, there's very little we need to subsist," she added. "We all know the basics: food, clothing, and shelter. But women who can't seem to distinguish between needs and wants actually talk themselves into believing that they really do *need* a pair of turquoise lizard pumps!"

In the following pages you'll meet three women—Julie, Suzanne, and Toni—who admit to confusion in their own lives about needs and wants. Each one has spent more money than she wants to. Each one is now facing the consequences of overspending. And each one has offered to share her story—to offer personal insight into the spending process and as a means of supporting her own recovery.

The Class Clown: Julie's Story

"I hate shopping, and I don't like to try on clothes," said Julie, a beautiful, middle-aged woman, the creator and president of a successful line of personalized gifts and novelty items that has recently gone nationwide. "I can go for a year without setting foot in a mall."

Yet, Julie, like millions of other women in debt, is an overspender. When she does shop she buys only the best, or the item with the most features or the highest price tag. "Apparently I think the more I spend, the better it is," she said, laughing.

When I asked her to share a little of her history regarding the subject of money, she tossed her head back and laughed again. "History, that's it. Whenever I have any money, it becomes history real fast."

I warmed up to her in seconds. She was open, easy to talk with, and quick-witted. I commented on her delightful sense of humor.

"Humor has kept me going my whole life," she said, "through an uncertain childhood, through two failed marriages, through a recent encounter with breast cancer."

Today it spills into her business. Among the novelty items Julie creates is a line of magnets for refrigerators and bulletin boards. Some of her favorites include a picture of a dog with the words "Fetch it yourself!" Others say, "Bus drivers tell you where to get off"; "Travel agents tell you where to go"; and "Journalists do it write."

As a child, Julie was nominated the class clown. "I was truly a person who was laughing on the outside but crying on the inside," she said on a wistful note.

The oldest of five children, Julie grew up in a two-bedroom bungalow in Detroit, Michigan. She remembers her father as a rageaholic—a person who was angry and suicidal his whole life. "I believe my dad was a genius," said Julie, "but he was not educated, and so he never reached his potential.

"We never had enough money," she said. "He spent a lot of his earnings on food for himself. He was a 350-pound over-eater who raided the refrigerator at night." Julie said this often meant the children went without milk and other break-fast food the next morning.

"We ate a lot of tuna casseroles in those days," she said, "and green beans. To this day I can't stand them. And I re-member eating ring bologna."

Julie's mother was a quiet person who did not stand up to her husband. The understanding was that he earned the money, so he could spend it however he wished. But Julie said she also remembers her father as a generous person in his own way—as long as he was the one to decide how the money would be spent.

Julie said her mother would cower in the corner when her husband had a rage attack. But when he was away she re-leased her feelings by yelling at the children. Julie believes that her own reckless attitude about life and her desire to take huge risks in relationships, with money, and with her business have resulted from her suppressed upbringing.

"I was the black sheep in the family," she added. "I pulled all the pranks. Even my dad laughed at some of them. I've always lived on the edge. I was a sky diver. I rode wild horses. I raced motorcycles. I even rode a motorcycle to work in downtown Detroit. I remember one day I knew I was going to be late for an important meeting, so I rode my motorcycle right into the building, took it on the elevator, and rode into the conference room. I got away with stuff like that. People expected it of me. They thought I was funny."

When Julie was a teenager she worked as a clerk at Kresge's five-and-dime store. "Every kid in the neighborhood looked forward to the day I got paid," she said. "They knew I'd bring them presents. I loved doing it. Buying for others was a form of power and control."

But that changed when Julie got in with a fast crowd. "Many of the others had money," she said, "and I began to see the difference between them and me. Some of the girls snubbed me because I didn't have a cashmere sweater or Capezio shoes. I think that was the first time I made a real distinction between myself and others," she said with a catch in her voice, then quipped, "Just when you catch up with the Joneses, they refinance."

Today, Julie is in debt—not a lot of debt, but more than she's comfortable with. "I'm ready to change," she said. "I want to go all the way with my recovery." She now keeps track of all her expenses, an important recovery tool suggested in the Twelve Step program Debtors Anonymous.

"I was shocked to find out that I spend about $100 a week on food," she added. "That's way too much for one person. But that's an indication of how I think. I usually buy the best-tasting or the most abundant whether in a grocery store or in a restaurant."

Even though Julie does not have heavy debts, she knows she's extravagant in ways that don't really satisfy her. For example, she says she'd rather play "big shot" around other people, buying them gifts and meals, than take care of some of her real needs. Because she hates to shop and loves to pay full price for her purchases, she tends to buy impulsively.

"I've spent nearly $300 on a three-month-old boy who's not even a relative. And I bought a $16 shirt for my employee's son just because I thought it was cute. It wasn't for any special occasion."

In addition, Julie said she gives things away without thinking. "If someone likes something I have, I give it to her. I also give away my time. At one point in my life I was volunteering up to twenty hours a week in addition to being a full-time real estate agent. I gave my blood. I gave out of guilt," she said soberly. "It seemed to help me deal with the shame of my childhood.

"I drive an eleven-year-old car, and I haven't been to a dentist in seven years. I went then only because it was an emergency. I haven't bought a business suit or a nice dress in the last ten years. Most of the time I run around in painter's pants and a crummy T-shirt, playing the starving artist."

When Julie does shop, she's fast and precise. For example,

after losing fifty pounds she decided to buy herself some new pants. "When I saw my size on the rack, I just closed my hand like an accordion over all eight or nine pairs, picked them up, and bought them. Yet I haven't worn some of them, and that was two years ago."

Another time Julie walked into a large chain variety store to buy some electrical tape. "One roll of black tape would have been fine," she said, "but no, I saw the various colors and decided I had to have two rolls of each color. I've never used them."

She says she has the same pattern with books. "If I see a book I like I buy several copies—one for my car, one for the bedroom, one to read on the plane when I take a trip." Interestingly, her latest multiple-book purchase was one on how to get out of debt!

Julie also has a surplus of 200 drawer dividers, the result of another overspending spree.

Her spending patterns and rituals are humorous on the surface. But to Julie they're not funny anymore. The pain of overspending and not taking care of herself has caught up with her, and she's working seriously now at her recovery program and her relationship with God.

"To the Manor Born": Suzanne's Story

"From the beginning my parents were mismatched," said Suzanne, a genteel, slow-speaking woman in her mid-sixties, as she reflected on the origins of her spending addiction. "My mother was terminally vague. My father made split-second decisions. So they never got together on anything."

Suzanne, the last of three children, was born when her parents were in their forties. They had lost their firstborn and almost lost Suzanne's sister to scarlet fever. "So I was raised delicately, raised to be spared," said Suzanne.

"My mother was a victim of what I call vignette thinking," she said. The term fascinated me, and I asked her to explain it. "She never saw the big picture. She'd see a dress or a pair of earrings or a painting, and immediately it would remind her of something else—some other time or experience, or it might be something she never had. She'd have to have it for my sister or me. She'd obsess about it until she bought it. We had

barrassed by this. As a result, she's had a
money."

dad was also a gambler, and everyone in the
it. He never gambled house money, so my
erfered. "He still gambles today," said Toni.
etired now and they take little trips to Atlan-
dad can gamble."

k over the years, Toni says her mother ex-
iving her food, and her father used money to
and money. That's the way I show myself
with an insightful chuckle, as deep dimples
n and open face.

ne, Toni received mixed messages from both
dad bought her things, but he also physically
en I was a kid he beat me whenever he got
iolent moods." But he is also the one who
portance of putting away ten cents from ev-
rned.

protected her husband yet also admitted
ould have left him if she had thought she
care of herself. Today her mother claims
n happy in her marriage.

parents have been to one or more of her
, and they've talked about the physical vio-
d denied that it was a problem. He told the
of Toni that she deserved it. She was a bad
nd he had to straighten her out!

ne, her parents are still supportive of her in
have given her money over the years when
and they don't press her for repayment. But
that it's important to her recovery to pay
lso understands that her dad's way of con-
loan or give her money.

experienced conflict over her upbringing in
rch. She entered a convent, "motivated to
he finished high school, and she remained a
ears. "At the time I thought it was the highest
way a person could live," she said. But that
years. "As a nun, I was a representative of
of life. I came out when I recognized that I no
be part of that."

everything we ever wanted and more. She also pushed us
ahead of our time—especially my sister. My mother wanted
her to date before she was ready."

Suzanne believes that some of the financial excess was also
due to the fact that her parents were older and had less energy for two active girls than younger people might have had.
Therefore, it was easier to give their daughters things than to
give them their time. "They never set limits," she said, "because they didn't want any stress. I could do anything I
wanted."

One thing Suzanne wanted was to wear braids and be a
tomboy. "I was allowed to be a tomboy," she said, reflecting
on her early years, "but I also had to take ballet lessons. My
dad was my best friend. He gave me everything from a horse
to riding lessons to the finest boarding school."

Suzanne truly felt that she was "to the manor born." But as
she grew up, she found the world was not as hospitable or as
eager to take care of her as her parents had been. "I remember I couldn't be around fast-moving people," she said, drawing out each word in soft, cultured tones. "For the first time in
my life I began to feel less than others. I couldn't get organized
that quickly."

Like her mother before her, she married a man who could
make decisions quickly and keep her and her sons organized.
He was a career officer in the Navy, so once again Suzanne
lived in an environment where she was totally cared for. The
Navy compound provided everything they needed. As a result, Suzanne admits, she never learned how to live in the real
world.

But amid the pampering and the plenty, her life was not
without tragedy. Her only sister committed suicide at age
thirty-eight, and her husband died while Suzanne was in her
mid-thirties. She was then faced with rearing her three boys
alone. "I had so much stress getting organized during those
years that I didn't want any more. So, like my parents, I never
set any boundaries for my sons. And I have no boundaries in
my life. All three of my boys have problems to this day because of it. In fact, our entire family has a history of mental
illness. It seems to be generational."

In the late 1980s, Suzanne put her family house on the market and planned to purchase a $300,000 condominium for her-

self and one of her sons who lives with her. But that purchase didn't work out, so she decided on a $500,000 house.

Reflecting on that time, she said with dismay, "Can you imagine? In a split second I jumped my expenditure by $200,000 without thinking, planning, or consulting anyone."

For years Suzanne has listened faithfully to Bruce Williams, a financial advisor on talk radio, yet when it came to making such an important decision as buying and selling a house, she did so without an attorney, CPA, or financial planner. "I did it on my own, and everything about it was wrong. The house is like a boat that has been under water for fifty years!"

For the first couple of years Suzanne put an enormous amount of money into fixing it up and restoring it instead of selling it. She says she's aware now that obsessing about the house took her mind off paying attention to the real problems in her life.

"I blank out when it comes to money," she admits. "I've spent $800 to $900 a month for a gardener for a house that's not even fit to live in. And I'm a soft touch for everyone else's needs. The gardener gave me a story about needing a new tire for his truck, so I bought him one. And on it goes.

"I see that I participate in unsatisfying activities to keep my mind off my pain. I remember hearing someone on a talk show saying that our activities take us away from the boredom of our own gray, depraved lives. That's absolutely true of me. I waste so much time and energy.

"For example, last summer one of my sons and his family said they might come and stay over a couple of nights. It wasn't definite, but that didn't matter. I went into a whirlwind of spending. I didn't have room for them in my condo so I decided to put them up at *the* house. It's empty—no furniture —and they could have used sleeping bags for the two nights, and then spent the days with me at the condo. But no, I was raised to think that a guest in your home is next to God. So I went out and spent $1,500 to $2,000 on beds and bedding so they'd have comfortable places to sleep. The beds are still there, the house hasn't sold, and my son's family never came."

Suzanne now sees her desire to be a gracious hostess as a way to continue obsessing about the house that hasn't sold. "It doesn't take much to stir me up," she said.

In May she was invite of her cousin's daughter ation," she said, "and n anything, just to come, itself. But no, I got over- buying more gifts than I couple of thousand doll fact, my cousin told me intended to give her da couldn't accept that. I e I took it to a profession that was another $150 other attempt to keep h what's really important.

"When my father died in investment scams. I di I got into things I didn't

Suzanne said she als such as long-distance ph "I call people who can't moods."

Suzanne is in recover gram, a women's thera church. "I still struggle changes. Like so many v wondering if I'm worth w

What Price Beauty: To

"I was called the smar hood, "and my cousin w I've been trying to buy be avoid my feelings."

Toni grew up in the Br "We weren't wealthy," sh remember thinking my fa ter closing his fruit and back injury, he held abo would always be able to sick. But my sister had

ashamed and en real drive to ear

Toni said her family accepted mother never in "My parents are tic City where n

In looking bac pressed love by show love. "Foc love," she said, creased her war

At the same ti her parents. Her abused her. "Wl into one of his taught her the i ery dollar she e

Toni's mother later that she v could have take she's always bee

Both of Toni' therapy session lence, but her d therapist in fron kid sometimes,

At the same ti many ways. The she's needed it, now she realize them back. She trolling her is to

Toni has also the Catholic Ch give all," when nun for sixteen and most perfec changed over th the Catholic way longer wanted t

Toni seems to have marched to a different drummer most of her life. Her years in the convent were no exception—even after she made her religious vows of poverty, chastity, and obedience. "Most nuns struggle with chastity and obedience," said Toni, "but I had a problem with poverty. Interestingly, that was the only vow that bothered me.

"I've always loved clothes," she said. "I'd rather have one $500 dress than five $100 dresses. I wanted the best. As a nun, it was hard for me to settle for living on a small allowance and wearing the same clothes over and over." And her mother's attitude during those years didn't help much. "She used to tell me that if I'd leave the convent she'd buy me a whole new wardrobe."

Toni also said she liked to associate with people who had money. "I even managed to be assigned to the wealthy parishes while I was a nun." But that mentality also made her feel guilty. "I knew Jesus had come to serve the poor, and here I was mingling with the rich. Later I noticed that the wealthy actually needed God more than the poor."

Toni told herself that if she ever left the religious order, she would never worry about money again. "When I finally did leave," she said, "I had $500 in my pocket—money I had earned on the side doing speaking engagements. I even managed to pay for my own car and was allowed to keep it when I left."

She was able to get a credit card right away, but she never abused it. In fact, at first she paid cash for most purchases. But then at some point, she said, "I lost all reality about money. I bought myself a house in New York and decorated it with the best. I had Laura Ashley everything! I put in a Jacuzzi™ and an English country garden. I learned to define myself by the money I spent."

She started her own computer training business in 1984 with a $10,000 start-up loan. Then she used her credit card to pay her employees' salary. That was the beginning of her dance with debt. "I had never been in debt before," she said. "I'd always had money for everything I needed."

When her debts began to mount, she held tight and didn't panic. "I had so many irons in the fire, I was sure something would pop. Then one thing happened after another. The business began to fold. She published a book for a friend and lost

$20,000 on that venture, then borrowed $28,000 from her parents. "I took money out of the business so I could look like a million," she said. "I didn't think I had a problem. It was the business. I also didn't want to look into it. I expected an accountant to keep track for me. I fired three of them!"

Toni has wanted someone to take care of her. "I'm very ill-at-ease around men," she said. "I've always chosen men who are unavailable. I still believe that my life won't really work until I lose enough weight, make enough money, and have the right man in my life. I keep telling myself that I'll be okay when these three things are in place."

Yet as much as she wants to be taken care of, she admits it's nearly impossible for her to receive. She prefers to give. "I buy lots of expensive gifts. I gave my secretary a pair of diamond earrings. I give presents worth a minimum of $100. Money has been my way of showing off. I feel that I should be the one paying at all times. But I never thought it was wrong because I also gave to myself."

In 1990 Toni made $90,000 giving speeches and seminars. Yet today she is $100,000 in debt. "My living expenses were $6,000 a month." As fast as the money came in, Toni used it to pay down her debts. That left her cash poor, and she'd use her credit cards again.

"In the last few months I have learned that the number-one way to get out of debt is to stop debting. That was a brand-new concept for me. It had never occurred to me before." Toni had used credit to pay off credit for so long that it had become a way of life.

When she moved to the West Coast, she was looking for a fresh start, a new way of viewing herself and others. "I'm beginning to learn that I'm not my money," she said, "but my life is still a puzzle, and I'm in the middle of it."

Toni's real gifts are in the area of teaching and public speaking, yet today she's working in a dress shop for $5 an hour. "I think I'm still in denial," she said, "because I can't see myself in this position. And I don't understand the mentality of women who view themselves as paupers and under-earners. When I feel ugly or bad, I go out and buy something for myself. Even when I don't have money, I find enough to treat myself to a nice meal. I guess there's a piece of me that doesn't believe I'll be this way forever."

Taking Inventory

Women who are overspenders answer "often" or "very often" to many of these statements:

1. I buy things I don't really need or want.

2. If I have money in my purse I feel I have to spend it.

3. I buy things even when I cannot afford them.

4. I spend money to make myself feel better.

5. I overspend on gifts to impress or gain the approval of others.

6. I buy things on sale—just because they're on sale.

7. I indulge in spending rituals such as buying in pairs.

8. I feel secretive about my spending habits.

4

Shopaholics

My aunt Janet fascinated me as I was growing up. She had the ability to produce, seemingly from nowhere, bathing suits of every size and color, blouses and shorts, socks and scarves. When she gave me a gift for a birthday or graduation, she urged me to slip into it right on the spot. If it was the wrong size or color or a style I didn't like, no problem. She'd fly off to one of the back rooms and return in an instant with a replacement. Or if she were visiting at our house, she'd run out to the car and do the same.

She apparently kept a stock of items on hand for all occasions and for all the people in her life. She had a family of six children and numerous nieces, nephews, sisters, in-laws, and friends. There was always someone to give something to. I don't recall the gifts ever being wrapped—just handed over. Her generosity pleased me, and her willingness to produce the perfect item each time continues to fascinate me.

I don't know if Aunt Janet was a shopaholic or simply a generous person who enjoyed shopping for family and friends. But I do know that she spent many hours poring over sales and buying items in bulk.

I also remember hearing stories about the mother of one of my childhood friends who went shopping *every day*. It was as much a part of her routine as cooking or gardening. She said it helped her relax. My friend was one of the best-dressed kids in our sixth-grade class. I had one pair of school shoes. She had four. I had one bathing suit. She had two or three.

When we met again years later I asked her if her mother was

still shopping. Her face sobered when she told me that her parents had gotten divorced while she was in college. Her mother had run up so much debt that they lost the family home, and in the end filed for bankruptcy.

My friend said she has the same problem with shopping, but when she saw it getting a grip on her life, she got into therapy to deal with it before she lost her family too.

THE PERFECT MARRIAGE

There is shopping—for food and clothing, a car and a house —in order to live. And there is living in order to shop—the kind of shopping where your heart beats faster as you approach the front door of your favorite department store, or your palms suddenly turn moist when you walk past a boutique with fabulous leather goods. And there are many places in between. Some women go on a spending binge for several days and then abstain for months. Others shop as a form of entertainment. They don't go into debt, but they enjoy walking through a mall and buying a few things as much as other women might enjoy a hike in the mountains or a couple of sets of tennis.

I sense that my aunt fit somewhere in the middle. She spent a lot of money on "stuff," but usually it was for other people. Somehow that made it respectable—even admirable. And my schoolmate's mother—well, by today's definition she might be considered a compulsive shopper.

Shopping and women, women and shopping. The perfect marriage. They go together like a horse and carriage. And our culture blesses the union. Women are expected to shop. Encouraged to shop. Wooed into shopping. That's a big part of the problem.

Even the term *shopaholic* is a "cutesy" take-off on the word *alcoholic*. But there is nothing cute about compulsive shopping. It is a serious addiction for millions of women, every bit as serious as drug, alcohol, or food abuse.

In 1986 American shoppers spent one trillion dollars, 54 percent in shopping centers. Seventy percent of the population is overextended with money or credit.

THE SHOPPING GENE

Compulsive shopping is particularly insidious because, unlike dark alley dysfunctions such as drugs and alcohol, shopping is pristine. Some men may have the disorder, but for the most part, behavioral experts agree that men lack the "shopping gene."

My son-in-law Bruce, for example, admits he could spend a day surfing, fixing the washing machine, and repairing his car and still feel great, but an hour in a mall and he's wiped out. He may also agree with the young man who told his girlfriend, in response to her invitation to go shopping, "If I want to hang out with clothes that have never been worn, I'll go sit in your closet for an hour!"

That statement is good for a laugh, but for compulsive shoppers like Maria, it's anything but funny. "I *have* to shop to feel good," she says. "It's the *shopping* itself that I like. It doesn't matter what I buy. In fact, the stuff usually looks great in the store, not so good the next day, and a week later it looks awful."

Maria sighed deeply and folded and unfolded her slender hands. "But I still do it. Then I hate myself and feel guilty. And to get rid of those feelings I go shopping again. It's one sick cycle, I know. But I can't seem to break it, no matter how many times I promise myself that this will be the last time.

"I have clothes in my closet that I've never taken out of the bag. The tags are still on a pair of pants I bought two years ago. Why don't I take the stuff back? I don't know. That's not fun. It's a hassle, and the clerks look at you like you're trying to rob their commission or something. Besides, what I really like is *shopping,* not returning things."

NO RESPECTER OF AGES

Shopping addiction hits hardest among young women. It is the perfect way for a good girl to act bad—without being judged for it. But age is no barrier. Shopaholics span all age groups. One eighty-seven-year-old great-grandmother has gone through her $50,000 inheritance in three years because she can't stop shopping. Confined to home because of arthritis, part of her entertainment is watching the Home Shopping Network on television.

Any woman can find a reason to justify a day at the mall, a quick stop at a boutique, a few items from the mail order catalogue, or an afternoon in front of the shopping channel.

Every woman needs clothes and equipment for work and school and sports and evenings out. Then there are gifts for others, the right car, and of course, the perfect accessory. Shopaholics are decent women—women who care about how they look and how they feel—but to an extreme.

A SYSTEM OF SHOULDS

Most shopping addicts are living out someone else's "should system"—their mothers', a celebrity's, a manufacturer's, a designer's, a friend's. They are dealing with psychological and social influences so great they cannot even consider them, much less face and deal with them. Issues of low self-esteem, lack of boundaries, and problems with reality are all part of the complex behavior that plays itself out in a shopping frenzy.

Compulsive shopping "fits the addictive cycle," said Elizabeth A. Edwards,[1] a graduate student at the University of Michigan, who is studying several hundred compulsive shoppers. In a recent media interview Edwards said the addictive process is involved when people shop to relieve tension and then find the need to shop again the next time they feel anxious. "And because the shopping itself intensifies pressures, it feeds on itself," she added.

Even our language supports this system of addiction. Cars boast bumper stickers such as "When the going gets tough, the tough go shopping" or "I'd rather be shopping." "Born to shop" is emblazoned on a coffee mug one of my daughters received as a gift. Even the expression "shopping spree" suggests out-of-control buying.

In addition, stores encourage shopping by featuring cafes and snack bars on the same floor as popular merchandise. Customers are invited to open a charge account so they can acquire a preferred rating. Free personal shopping services are available for women who want a professional clothing consultant to help coordinate a wardrobe or a special outfit.

None of these services of itself is bad. Some of them are even helpful and certainly convenient. I have enjoyed using a personal shopper, and when I did use department store credit cards I found them a wonderful convenience. I could do all my shopping in one day, in one place, without having to write individual checks in each department. At the end of the month I'd write one check for the entire purchase and bring my balance back to zero. That worked for me, because compulsive shopping is not my thing.

But to a person who is easily addicted the colors, textures, jewelry, books, clothing, and cosmetics in a row of stores and boutiques are as seductive as potato chips. Bet you can't buy just one. Compulsive shopping has been the cause of marriages breaking up, hospitalization, bankruptcy, theft, and a host of other maladies that suck the very life out of the women who drop by the mall "to pick up a few things."

Compulsive shopping is not just the domain of those who wish to keep up appearances or those who are material-minded. There are shopaholics of every nationality, background, and belief. Women with strong spiritual convictions are just as likely to be found pounding the pavement of a mall as someone who believes in living just for today.

One Christian woman said she justifies her shopping addiction by limiting herself to Christian bookstores and church thrift shops. "I buy books and bumper stickers and music tapes and T-shirts for my grandkids and greeting cards and on and on. As long as it's got a spiritual angle, I find a way to rationalize buying it. But now that I'm in Overcomers Outreach—a Christian support group for people with addictions —I see how much I've been kidding myself."

Kim Hong emigrated with her family to the United States from Vietnam during the mid-1970s when she was fifteen. She remembers being overwhelmed by the large supermarkets and grocery stores. "At first I was afraid to go shopping," she said. "But now I'm a—what do you call it—shopaholic. I want everything I see. We were very poor when I was growing up and, of course, in Vietnam during the war years, we didn't have the opportunity to do anything but survive."

Now in her mid-thirties, Kim has her own beauty salon, her

own money, and her own life. "It's as though I am trying to make up for all those years when I had nothing, not even a pair of shoes. But you make it so easy in this country to go into debt. I think it's wrong. Now I am working hard to pay back what I owe—$10,000. Even though I owe so much money, I still find things I want to buy. I love to shop. The stores here are so beautiful."

THE GREAT COVER-UP

There are as many ways to shop compulsively as there are women who do it. But one thing most appear to have in common is a need to fill the emptiness they feel inside. One thirty-two-year-old executive secretary in Beverly Hills, California, reported that the night before Valentine's Day one year she and her boyfriend had a fight. She knew there would be no flowers or candlelight dinner for her the next day.

"That morning my feelings of anger and resentment were so strong all I could think to do was shop. If he doesn't love me, then I can love myself, I thought. During my lunch hour I marched right over to Rodeo Drive and charged a $1,000 watch I had been wanting for months. Then I walked back to work and started typing as if I had just bought a $10 bracelet."

Another compulsive shopper said she spends her money on other people to keep relationships going. "I have a birthday book that rivals the Yellow Pages," she said, laughing. "I'm absolutely nutty about remembering people's birthdays. I spend so much money on Hallmark products they ought to make me a stockholder. I lose all sense of reality in a stationery store. I pick up cards like most people pick up groceries. It's nothing for me to drop $25 to $50 at a time."

Powerlessness, low self-esteem, insecurity in relationships, and stress on the job are common factors that trigger compulsive shopping. But the roots of these feelings are much deeper, as shown in the stories of the following four women. Most of these feelings can be traced to specific childhood experiences, events, and situations where a young girl received unhealthy messages about her physical and emotional needs around money.

The Fur Muff: Georgia's Story

Georgia learned early in life that money could stimulate her emotions. Her father was a traveling salesman for a book company during the late forties. When sales were up he'd come home with presents for everyone. "I especially remember a little brown fur muff he gave me to warm my hands," said Georgia, a tall, slender brunette. "I was about seven at the time, and it was the most wonderful present I could ever imagine. It was all the more special because my dad picked it out just for me."

But when sales were down and commissions low, so were her father's emotions. "He'd come in the door and barely speak to any of us. Then my mother would scurry around shushing us kids and waiting on Dad hand and foot, trying to win him back. I went right along with her. But when I think of it now, it makes me sick," she added, frowning.

"He ran the show—from the road. Today he'd be considered an absentee father. And yet his power over our household was so strong, you'd think he was there twenty-four hours a day."

Georgia, in an interesting recreation of her past, also works in sales. Single at forty-eight, she lives out of a suitcase most of the time and spends many hours alone, driving from one city to another. At night she often eats alone, then ends her day by walking through a mall.

"If I'd just browse, it'd be fine," she said, "but it never stops there. I always find something I absolutely *have* to have. I'm never bored because I'm in different cities several days a month.

"To me a shopping mall is like a carnival," said Georgia. "I get absolutely high with the colors and textures and displays. Clothes are my downfall." I could tell by looking at her, dressed in an elegant purple silk suit with a lovely print blouse and large chunky silver bracelet and earrings. "I have enough clothes to start my own boutique," she said, laughing in embarrassment. "In fact, my best friend tells me I ought to start a resale clothing store since my own stock could keep me going for a year," she said, with a catch in her voice.

"If it weren't so pathetic, I'd laugh—and maybe I'd even consider it. But it's not funny anymore. I'm a shopping junkie.

I've gotten over my food addiction and I no longer drink. But I can't stop shopping.

"I also have a thing about being on mailing lists. I sign up at every store. It makes me feel important to be a preferred customer, to be one of the people who hears about the sales and promotions before the rest of the world. I guess it's like the feeling I had when my dad gave me the fur muff. I was special. I had a muff before any of my friends had one."

Georgia's mother was a quiet person, but she, too, loved to shop. When things got steamy around the house, her mother rounded up the girls—Georgia and her two sisters—and took them shopping on Mason Avenue—a street in their town lined with shops and boutiques, five-and-ten cent stores, and ice cream parlors.

"My mother would buy us each a little something—maybe a bow for our hair or a new pair of socks 'to cheer you up,' she'd say. Then we'd stop for a soda or ice cream. Afterward we went home, and things seemed calmer somehow. I think I began to associate shopping with feeling good and with taking away the loneliness I felt so much of the time while growing up."

Today, Georgia owes $15,000 to department stores and credit card companies. She's in therapy for the issues that have fueled her addiction, and she's seeking help from Consumer Credit Counselors. "I feel hopeful for the first time in my life," she said, flashing her deep brown eyes. "I need help, and I'm willing to receive it."

Never Enough: Ann's Story

Ann's shopping addiction is also rooted in her childhood. She was the only girl and eldest of six children. "My parents were ultraconservative fundamentalist Protestants, and my father believed a woman's place was in the home, at least while the children were young." The fact that he earned very little as a college professor did not change his view.

Ann's mother continued to get pregnant, because "she believed it was God's will," despite the fact that she was Rh negative. "That meant she was confined to bed at the beginning of the second trimester of each pregnancy to prevent premature birth. It also meant that I reared my brothers."

money—for food and clothing and survival—came from the men in my life."

Today Ann is sorting out her wants and needs and coming to terms with her fear and shame around finances, and the harmful messages she received about God's teachings on money.

I'll Take Two: Esther's Story

Esther is also a compulsive shopper, but unlike Georgia and Ann, Esther buys in pairs. "I can *never* buy just one of anything," said the brunette in her late thirties. "I remember shopping with my Jewish grandmother who raised me, and she always bought more than one—from bagels to chickens," she said.

"She had what I call an emergency philosophy. She was always preparing for a crisis. If I were buying a candy bar, she'd say, 'Buy two, honey, in case you get hungry later.' If I saw a blouse or skirt I liked, she'd urge me to get two—one for good wear and one for everyday, or one for now and one for later. She planned ahead to the point of obsession. 'What if it breaks or gets lost or somebody steals it?' she'd ask. 'You'll have a second one, and you won't worry.' "

Esther said this compulsive process drove her crazy. They had two can openers, two toasters, two cookie jars, and so on. Later, when Esther was living on her own, she found herself shopping in the same compulsive way. Debt was not as much of a problem for her as the ritual of shopping for pairs.

"You should see my house," she said, laughing self-consciously. "You wouldn't believe the collection of weird stuff I have. Two cans of paint, when one is enough, two sets of dishes, though I live alone, two irons, two this, two that. I hate it, but somehow I feel incomplete if I buy just one of something. I find myself remembering my grandmother's warning that I'll be sorry if I have only one and it breaks or gets lost or is stolen. I have so much junk I wish someone *would* steal a few things. I don't use half the stuff I buy."

Esther's ritualistic shopping also stands in the way of planning or saving for anything meaningful. "For example, I've never taken a real vacation since I started working over ten years ago. And I don't have any play clothes. I recently discovered while sharing in my therapy that I don't have these things because I think I don't deserve to play. With a crisis just around the corner, who has time for fun? That was a real breakthrough for me.

"My grandmother believed in hard work, nose-to-the-grindstone kind of thing. Even though shopping was an outlet for her, she bought only things that made sense to her—and then she bought two so she'd never be without."

Esther finds she has the same odd mixture of values. "I buy serviceable items—in pairs, of course," she said, laughing. "But they never really satisfy me. And because I buy two of everything I don't have enough money to buy something I really want—like a pure silk blouse or a genuine leather purse."

Esther, like other compulsive shoppers, is also a woman in debt. "It's not a lot by most standards, but it's crippling *me,*" she said, poking herself in the chest as if to make a point, "especially the interest payments. I feel like I'll be paying for can openers and plastic potato chip bag clips for the rest of my life. I can't seem to leave a mall without charging something or using up every bit of money I have in my wallet."

She shifted her gaze for a moment and then continued softly as if to apologize. "I rarely buy big items like a lamp or a chair or a bed. I fritter away my money on little things. That's how I keep myself stuck. Then when a friend invites me to a movie or to go away for a weekend, I tell her I can't afford it. The truth is I don't think I deserve to take a day off when I have so much debt. I should be working to pay it off."

No More Hand-me-downs: Roberta's Story

Roberta was born in Los Angeles of Hispanic parents, the last of six children. "We never lacked for food," she said, a beautiful, dark-eyed woman of thirty-nine. "But I never had many clothes, and most of what I did have were hand-me-downs from my older sisters. My dad was a workaholic and an alcoholic. And he was very tight with his money, except when it came to my mother. He bought her many gifts—new cars, expensive jewelry—and he had her clothes made for her."

Because her father was the dominating one in the family as well as the disciplinarian, Roberta grew up depending on him.

She never learned to take care of herself. Whenever she and her siblings needed anything they had to ask their dad for it and justify why it was necessary. "I grew up expecting others to take care of me," she admitted. "I never learned to save, never planned for the future or for my retirement."

As an adult when she spent money on herself, Roberta felt wonderful. "I saw it as a way of taking care of myself," she said. "I also spent it so I wouldn't have to share it. No matter how much I had, I'd get rid of it. I was afraid to buy anything tangible or I might have to share it with someone else." Instead, she bought consumable items such as books, airline tickets, and gifts.

Roberta was married twice. "I married the first man because I knew he'd be a good provider and I'd be secure. But I didn't love him." She soon discovered that he had all the characteristics of her father. "He was traditional, tight with money, and very controlling. I hid all my purchases from him."

Eight years after her divorce, Roberta married again. "It was for love," she said. "He was an artist, and I thought it would be different this time. In a way it was. In this relationship *he* was the debtor. I had reversed the roles. He was looking for someone to take care of him!"

Roberta had credit cards, and she let him use them. After two years they divorced, and she was left with $10,000 to $12,000 of debt. "He ruined my credit," she said, "and I was forced to step down in my life. I moved to a dinky apartment in order to save enough money to pay back the debts."

But Roberta discovered after her second divorce that her own problem with shopping and spending was not over. Her cycle of debt erupted again. "I knew I was in trouble, because I knew my income and I was uncomfortable with how much I'd spent." Roberta buys clothes, presents, meals, and odds and ends she doesn't really need—anything to keep the money out of her hands and away from her bank account. "I have used shopping and spending as proof that I can take care of myself."

Over the years Roberta has stopped her compulsive shopping for as much as five years at a time, but eventually returned to it. This stop-and-start mode is a family pattern, she admits. "My father did the same thing with alcohol," she said. "He'd stop for a time and then start again."

Roberta knows that her dysfunction with money is a reflection of her childhood emotional deprivation. "I've always had this desire to be special in my family," she said. "Shopping, spending, charging on credit cards came in on that level. It gave me a sense of power."

Today Roberta is engaged to be married again, and she admits that she has a lot of fear around the topic of marriage as well as money. "We went to look at rings," she said, "and that shopping experience sent me on an emotional roller coaster. I realized how things can sneak up on me if I'm not aware and conscious of each moment. A week after I received the ring, my fiancé came over and basically said, 'Where's dinner?'" Roberta laughed at the implication. The old male-female dynamic dies hard.

"I began noticing subtle messages from the past that told me I can't have a career and be married," she said. The fear of being controlled and changed and manipulated began to haunt her again. Roberta remembers as a child living in fear of being controlled—by her father, by men, by money, and by the nuns in the Catholic school she attended.

Today she is working through the fear, the messages, and the patterns, and she is looking within to find out what God has for *her*, Roberta, today. One thing she seems sure of is that there will be no more hand-me-downs.

Taking Inventory

Women who are compulsive shoppers answer "often" or "very often" to many of these statements.

1. Shopping is my most common form of entertainment.

2. I feel anxious when I am not shopping.

3. Shopping takes the place of talking and feeling and dealing with the unpleasant realities of my life.

4. I argue with others about my shopping and spending habits.

5. I repeatedly buy things I neither need nor want.

6. I get a rush or a high from the shopping process or even thinking about it.

7. I am concerned about how often I shop, but I continue to shop anyway.

8. I minimize my purchases or hide them from my family.

9. I buy clothing that does not fit my lifestyle—evening gowns, aerobic wear, or dance shoes—when I rarely, if ever, use them.

Credit Card Abusers

Credit cards are as foreign to Gina's present lifestyle as hamburgers are to a vegetarian. But it was not always that way. At one time Gina owed nearly $25,000 in credit card debt. She had three bank cards and two department store cards, and each one was filled to the limit. It took her five years at a second job to pay off the debt. "I'll never put myself through that again," she said, despite the fact that the creditors continue to entice her with new cards and higher limits—because of her "excellent record."

Gina knows differently now. The credit card companies are not as interested in her payment performance as they are in the interest they earn on her installments, as she learned from her brother who works in a bank.

Recently this truth came home to her again when she purchased a winter coat for $250 at a large department store in Manhattan. As the clerk rang up the sale, she asked, "May I put this on your credit card?"

Gina declined, saying she preferred to pay cash. She handed the clerk a $500 bill. But the clerk did not have sufficient change on hand, so she called customer service to have it delivered to her department. The episode dragged on for fifteen minutes, and Gina became impatient waiting. She asked the clerk to investigate the delay.

The woman called upstairs again and was apparently told to discourage customers from paying cash. She told Gina that management preferred shoppers to use the store card, but that someone would be down in a moment with her change. "I never thought I'd see the day when cash was more of a hassle than credit," said Gina.

As they waited, the young clerk took it upon herself to educate Gina about management's goals. "Credit cards are easier for everyone," she offered, in a buoyant attempt to change Gina's viewpoint. "The customer doesn't have to wait. You don't have to pay your balance for a month, and if you're a little short, you can pay over time. And it's good for the store too," she added. "We make money on the interest from those who prefer to use our installment plan."

"I've been that route," Gina told the clerk, with a note of disgust in her voice. "And I don't intend to go back. I ran up so much debt I was on the verge of bankruptcy, suicide, or both. No thanks!"

"But the store knows some people won't pay," said the clerk, brightly. "With a 21 percent interest rate we can afford to let some accounts slide. Management takes that into consideration when they price the items," she added confidently.

"That sounds like a sneaky way of saying they raise their prices to cover the deadbeats, and also make a nice profit off people like me, who prefer to pay cash." Gina left the store, coat in hand, change in her purse, and a whole lot wiser.

In talking about it later, she said she wasn't proud of her sour tone, but frankly, she was angry at how simple the clerk had made it sound. "Plastic is poison," she added, "and no amount of sugar coating will make it palatable."

CREDIT CARD MANIA

Gina is not alone. Since the mid-seventies credit cards have created more litter than have plastic cups on the beach. According to the *U.S. News and World Report* May 6, 1991 issue, after taxes, interest, and pension contributions, household debt rose from 80 percent in 1980 to 110 percent in 1989. Interestingly, from 1975 to the present, credit card use also exploded in our culture. *Forbes* magazine noted in March 1986, that Americans carried 720,000,000 credit cards, and their use was expanding.

Today we are almost forced to use credit cards for everything from renting a car to ordering a piece of merchandise over the phone. Those who balk and say "No thanks, I'll pay cash" or "I don't use credit cards" or "I'll send a check with my order form" are considered aliens. And indeed we are. What self-respecting American woman would actually leave home without her American Express, Visa, or Mastercard?

Credit card abuse is not just a once-in-a-while binge, such as eating too many chocolate pecan truffles or buying three pairs of pantyhose when one would do. It's a disorder—as widespread and compulsive as any other behavior addiction, from gambling to watching TV. And studies conducted by credit card companies show how easily the disorder is triggered. A report from Consumer Credit Counseling Service indicates that using credit cards increases spending by 34 percent.

COMPANION AND CONFIDANT

Women who cling to cards, however, are not necessarily overspenders or compulsive shoppers. For many it isn't the process of shopping or spending that gives them the rush. It's the card itself.

Many credit card abusers I spoke with said the card seems to take on an identity of its own. It is more than a convenient means of paying for a purchase. It becomes a companion and confidant, much like cigarettes or alcohol to the addicted smoker or drinker, and it appears to provide power and opportunity that many women feel unable to produce on their own.

Escape to the future

Letty said she finds that using credit cards tends to keep her from living in the present. "As soon as I charge a dress or a lunch or an airline ticket, I immediately start thinking about how I'm going to pay for it. I'm just sure things will be better tomorrow, next week, or next month. Maybe I'll get a raise. Or I look ahead to money I'll receive for my birthday or Christmas or the bonus at the end of the year. I tell myself I'll wipe out all my credit card debt then, and somehow it makes perfect sense to me at the time."

Avoidance of reality

Twenty-three-year-old Kit received her first bank card the same year she went to work as a clerk in a hotel. She didn't make much at first, but was promised a promotion and a raise after six months. "That was all the incentive I needed," she said. "I decided to use my card for stuff I clearly couldn't afford—like clothes and gifts and a weekend vacation. I figured that as long as I was making minimum payments I was fine. It wasn't until one of my friends told me she thought I had a problem with credit cards that I started to look at it. I never considered the entire bill my responsibility—just the minimum payments."

Mitzi said she avoided reality in a different way. "I only used my Visa card to shop sales," she said, stressing the past tense. "That was a real trap, though. I'd figure I was saving so much —maybe 20 percent to 50 percent—that I could afford to charge it. But then I saw that I was losing touch with the real cost of the item because I put so much attention on what I was saving. It was really crazy."

Comfort and companionship

Maureen said she feels like "somebody" with a credit card. "It helps me cope with living alone," said the single, forty-two-year-old secretary. "My card can always take me somewhere or buy me something when I'm down."

Many women agree that they start feeling as though they *deserve* special treatment every time they experience a change in mood or a disappointment. To Maureen the credit card assumes the role of a father, mate, or friend who will take care of her. She looks to her credit cards for comfort and companionship instead of seeing them for what they are: a medium of exchange for goods purchased.

When the bill arrives the following month, Maureen, and others like her, is shocked to discover what she owes. One woman said she actually felt betrayed by her Mastercard!

Excitement

For Betty using a credit card has allowed her to purchase things she could never afford if she had to pay cash. "I like going to the shops along Michigan Avenue," said the Chicago waitress. "I pick out a dress or a pair of shoes and put it on my card like I was somebody. And when the salesgirl sees my card, she asks if she can put me on her mailing list. I like that —being a preferred customer at all those fancy places."

Vera woke up to her credit card abuse when she reached the limit of both her Visa and Discover cards. "I was mad at them," she said, laughing. "Can you believe it? It was as if those cards were human beings, responsible for hurting me. After talking it over with a friend I understood what I had been doing. I used to go to my dad as a kid whenever I needed money. If he said no, I'd get mad and go to my grandfather or my uncle. I was doing the same thing with my cards. When one would get maxed out, I'd get angry, throw it in a drawer, and go to another one."

Buying love and approval

Ellen, a thirty-three-year-old widow with two young sons, uses her credit cards when she's feeling sorry for her boys. "They don't have a dad, and I guess I'm trying to take his place by buying them whatever I think they should have— things their dad would have bought, like a football or a skateboard. I don't want them to forget him, and I guess I think this will help keep his memory alive. But I'm beginning to see it doesn't make sense."

GAMES PEOPLE PLAY WITH CREDIT CARDS

Credit card abusers also admit to playing every kind of mind game imaginable in order to keep their true feelings down and their merry-go-round of debt going.

Gift certificate game

Chrissy uses her bank card to charge a gift certificate at a department store. She then chooses an item of lesser value than the certificate and takes the cash difference to spend elsewhere or to make a payment on her outstanding balance.

Ruth plays a variation of the same game. She charges a gift certificate, uses it to purchase an item, then returns it the next day at a branch store and gets the cash, which she promptly spends on yet another item.

Shop till you drop game

Paula says her credit card spending is equivalent to a marathon. "I go on an all-out shopping spree in Palm Springs, charging as fast as I can walk. By the following morning I'm bored with the whole thing, can't stand what I purchased, feel ashamed, and end up returning the entire batch."

Peer approval game

Franny uses her credit cards to keep up appearances. "I charge a couple of things whenever I shop with a friend," she said. "But most of the time I take them back the next day. I just want to be part of the shopping spree. It's too embarrassing to admit I don't even like to shop that much."

I'll put it on my card game

This is a familiar game to many women who meet friends for lunch or dinner. Nina, for example, charges the meals on her card and collects cash from each individual. Then she has money to spend on other items.

Rob Visa to pay Mastercard game

Marta plays a variation on the old bill paying method of robbing Peter to pay Paul. "I get a cash advance from Visa and use it to make a payment on my Mastercard," she said. "I'm exhausted from all this game-playing, and nobody wins except the bank. I've been doing it for years. When I think of all the energy and time I've wasted chasing money or running from it, I'm absolutely sick. And yet I can't imagine life without my credit cards. There are so many emergencies I couldn't handle if I weren't able to charge them."

Credit card abuse, like other compulsive behaviors, does not suddenly overtake a person. It results from a unique combination of social influence and family messages and patterns, as Laurel, Joyce, and Valerie discovered during their recovery process from credit card abuse.

Little Girl Blue: Laurel's Story

"My dad was a general in the Marine Corps," said Laurel, a tall, striking blond in her mid-forties, an artist and a researcher for agencies that compile statistics on various social issues. "To my mother and me, he was *god*. He was the source of money and everything else.

"I was an only child, and yet most of my childhood I felt deprived. I remember getting only one dress for an entire school year. My father was very tight with money in most ways, but then he'd spoil me in other ways. We had to ask him —beg him, actually—for everything. Even my best act got me only half of what I needed."

For years, even as an adult, Laurel felt like a little girl whenever she went to her father for financial help. "I had to be practically destitute and emotionally distraught to get a response. It was humiliating. I don't go to him for money anymore."

Laurel's mother didn't dare cross her dad, but Laurel does remember that when he got a little too high-handed her mother would salute him sharply, and that would bring him back to reality.

"One of my earliest memories about my own relationship with money," said Laurel, "is from the time I was around the age of four or five. I had stolen some candy or gum, and I was caught and punished. Apparently I thought that was the only way to get what I wanted.

"It was absurd to even think that I could make money," she said. "My dad was the only one who could earn, and my mother and I knew it."

By the time Laurel reached high school, she returned to stealing to meet her needs. "In fact," she shared, with an embarrassed chuckle, "I stole so many clothes that one year I was voted the best-dressed girl in my class." When I asked her how she handled this with her parents, she said they didn't pay much attention to her, and if her mother did notice an outfit Laurel told her it was borrowed from a friend. Once again, stealing seemed like her only option. "I couldn't earn the money I needed," she said. "Only men could do that."

Laurel admits this is a belief that still runs her today. Even though she has had to work since her divorce more than fifteen years ago, she still doesn't believe she's capable of earning enough to *really* take care of herself. "I like being a little girl." There is still a part of her that enjoys the role of a needy child.

Laurel thinks that sometimes she actually likes to feel pain, to be a martyr, to be helpless. She said that taking responsibility for herself financially is one of the greatest challenges she has faced. Giving up drinking and drugs was easy compared to giving up her financial dependence on credit.

"I've always looked at jobs as an interim activity between my relationships with men. I don't take myself seriously as an earner," she added. Over the years, Laurel has been a waitress, an underwater diver, a private detective, and an insurance investigator. "I went through men like a box of tissues. Falling in love produced a chemical high—much like drugs or alcohol might. It was wonderful. But then I'd wake up, and it'd be over—just like that. I went on like this for years because I had no one to talk to, no one to give me a reality check."

Three years ago Laurel let go of her last relationship. She had finally begun to recognize her unhealthy dependence on men and realized she would never grow up as long as she had a man to take care of her. She decided to stay out of relationships for at least a year.

Exit men. Enter credit cards. "That's when I started using credit cards to support myself. I have four cards, and they're all maxed out." Still Laurel's credit rating is very important to her, so she always pays at least the minimum payment on time. She has also figured out ways to get the most mileage from her cards. One way is to charge at the end of the billing period. Then she has a month before the bill comes.

Laurel's biggest problem is under-earning, yet she also sees her credit cards as one of the ways to keep herself stuck in low-paying positions. "They're always there, always available. I can't imagine cutting them up," she said. "I honestly don't think I abuse them. I use them to survive."

In recent months, Laurel has been in treatment for depression—a condition she discovered while working the Debtors Anonymous program. "I think I've been depressed my whole life. But I'm learning now that the problem is inside me. My attitude determines my feelings. A litany of hate runs through me. I want to change that." Laurel also wants to find a job she loves and is good at. "It's depressing to do what I hate."

During a break between research assignments last year, Laurel had a couple of months to do whatever she wanted. She gave herself permission to paint. "Something happens at my easel," she said, "that doesn't happen anyplace else. The act of painting is so much of who I am that it alone is fulfilling." But when she had to go back to work, the old feelings of inadequacy and depression settled in again. "I need a new direction, a new way of thinking. I'm praying for help from God to find my creative side and a way to earn money using my creativity."

Financial Fantasyland: Joyce's Story

Joyce has a secret that is eating her alive both emotionally and mentally. She has run up over $10,000 on credit cards in one year and has no way to pay off the debt. She claims she can't tell her husband, because he'd be devastated. He leaves the bill-paying to her and takes pride in her ability to keep them "out of hot water."

"It's really strange," said Joyce, leaning forward as she talked, her gray-brown eyes intent on the napkin she continually folded and unfolded. "I never spend cash. I'm terrified of it. I can't seem to keep money in my wallet. If I have it, I spend it. A credit card looked like the perfect solution for me. I told myself that each month when the bill came I'd be able to see exactly what I'd bought, and that listing would keep me accountable. But in the past year exactly the opposite has happened. I always need something, and the plastic is—well, it's always there. I'm used to it. I realize now that I've been charging everything from a $3 snack at the deli to a $250 dress at Bonwit's.

"When I get the bill at the end of the month I'm floored at what I see. Half the time I don't even remember where I was or how much I spent. I vow I'm going to slow down, but then the pattern starts all over again.

"Plastic money seems to be my substance of choice." She continued, laughing nervously. "Not that I'm some kind of addict. But I know it's gotten out of hand. I'm a wreck every morning—scared to leave the house until the mail arrives for fear my mother or my husband will get to it first and see what I've done. I've got to find a way to handle this without telling Tom."

Joyce began using credit cards the year she graduated from college and got her first job and apartment. "The application for my first one appeared in the mailbox one day, unsolicited. I thought to myself, wow, here's a bank that trusts me more than my own father does. I can handle this. At the time my credit limit was only $300, but it seemed like the moon to me. I was making only $18,000 a year at the time.

"It felt like a pass to Disneyland. Suddenly so many of the things I had always wanted and needed were within reach. But at the same time it scared me. It seemed to have a power all its own. I put it in a drawer for a while and kept it there, to be used for special occasions only—like Christmas gifts or a major car repair. I had always been terrified of debt. My parents filed for bankruptcy when I was in high school, and I remember the shame I felt when I found out."

Joyce looked down for a moment in thought, then continued. "But before long, my needs and wants got all mixed up, and I started taking out that card more and more often. Pretty soon I carried it with me every day—in case of emergency, I told myself. But I seemed to create one emergency after another. It was a pass all right—a pass to Financial Fantasyland."

By the end of that year, Joyce was $1,000 in debt. Her credit limit was raised, and again she charged to the limit. "I was frantic. Finally I confided in my mother's sister, an aunt I had been close to throughout my childhood. She was single and frugal, and everyone said she had a pile of money stashed away. I asked her for a loan. She said no to the loan, then

...ed her iced tea, then leaned forward and said in a
..., "The difference between my mother and me is
...er went into debt to get what she wanted. My
...ayed a lot."

...ecka resented her mother because the beauty
...urch seemed more important to her than her
...guess that's not fair," said Becka, leaning back in
...hen I look back now she was a young widow with
...d a young child to support. I'm sure she was
...f the time. She did the very best she could under
...ances. But for a long time I couldn't set foot in a
...mad at God for getting more of my mom's atten-
...t."

...rned to her story of her descent into debt. "The
...et me, but the creditors finally did." Representa-
...edit card companies and banks started calling.
... Then an IRS agent called about her unpaid back
...as though I was being sucked into a black hole,"
...nging her hands absently.

...the first time in my life I actually considered sui-
...'t see any way out. I had forgotten every positive
...ver learned. I couldn't call anyone. I didn't know
...o have fun.

...'t know where I'd be today if God hadn't inter-
...iraculous way," added Becka. "A friend of mine
...seen in years came down from Los Angeles, and
...reakfast. I don't know what came over me," said
...something snapped. When she asked how I was
...e down and told her the whole story.

...ed across the table and said, 'Becka, I under-
...than you might know.' Then she scribbled a
...er on a napkin and passed it across the table.
...nber. It's a support group for people in trouble

... That was my introduction to Debtors Anony-
...ram that has essentially helped me turn my life
...round. I'm still in debt, but I did sell my house
...some of the profits to pay my taxes and some of
...es. I turned in my leased car and bought a two-
...da—just as comfortable for my clients as my for-
...and a lot less expensive.

wrote me a check for a $1,000—'a big birthday present,' she said with a twinkle in her eye. But she made me promise to get rid of my card, and above all not to tell my mother because it would kill her to have a daughter in debt too."

Joyce ran a hand through her hair as if she were reliving the emotions of that day. "I'll never forget the relief I felt. I deposited the money, paid off my card, and cut it in half. I stayed debt free for several months—until the renewal card arrived in the mail. Once again, I put it in my wallet for emergencies. But the cycle started again. Within a year I was in debt again—this time for $3,000.

"I knew I couldn't go to my mother or my aunt. So I got a second job, waitressing banquets on the weekend. I stopped charging and paid off the $3,000 in a year. By that time offers for other cards came in the mail. I said yes to two more.

"But I still didn't see the sick pattern—until I married Tom two years later. He was so impressed with my record keeping and my eye for a bargain that he put me in charge of our finances right away. For the last three years I've handled everything except our taxes. It's been a nightmare. I put on a good show, but the truth is I'm a kid when it comes to credit."

When Joyce looks back on her childhood, she's reminded of many strange patterns connected with money. "There seemed to be a hush-hush atmosphere around financial affairs. To this day I have no idea what my father earned. I don't remember either my mother or my dad teaching me anything about money. A boyfriend in college showed me how to balance my checkbook. I'm a whiz at that now. In fact, I'm great at record keeping of all kinds. But I lack financial savvy. I don't have a grasp of the big picture—how to save and invest and when to spend and when not to."

Joyce and her husband rarely discuss money, and they have no long-term financial plan. "He loves the fact that I'm doing something he hates to do. He likes teaching and reading. His material needs are few, and he has only one hobby—fishing—that requires any money."

I noticed Joyce's eyes water as she talked about her feelings. "I'm so ashamed when I think of how I've let him down, and he doesn't even know it yet. It's pointless to blame my parents at this stage of my life. They did the best they could.

They were hard-working people, sacrificed a lot for my sister and me, and probably didn't know a whole lot more about money at the time than I do now. It's time for me to grow up, to face Tom, and to get some help. I don't want to live like this anymore."

Credit Card Cancer: Becka's Story

Forty-eight-year-old Becka is the kind of woman who still turns heads. Her elegant dress, generous smile, and almost regal appearance capture everyone who meets her. But Becka, like thousands of other women in debt, has had a serious and long-term bout with what she calls "credit card cancer."

It started during the mid-eighties when her once-prosperous real estate business began to spiral downward as it did for many agents and brokers throughout California. Becka said she had made over $100,000 several years in a row during the real estate boom in the seventies, so she did not panic when the market softened. "I had always been a survivor, and I knew I always would be. Several of my friends got out before they lost everything, but I didn't want to throw away a career that had been a good thing for so long. I told myself to sit tight, trust, and hang on."

The first crisis hit when two of her best agents left her office. "My uncertain income plummeted immediately, and yet my overhead remained essentially the same," said Becka, gazing at the Pacific Ocean across the highway from her San Clemente condominium.

"Times were tough for everyone, but as a broker I really felt it. It was then I started abusing credit cards. I had always used them, but for the most part I paid my bills on time. I never had a serious problem with debt until 1986. Instead of cutting back when things were uncertain, I went the other way. I couldn't let myself rest."

Becka said she was determined to turn her business around and to keep up appearances. She refinanced her house, then completely redecorated it and installed a Jacuzzi™.

"My payments for these loans took half my earnings," she said, "so I began putting clothes and meals and business expenses on my bank cards. It was nothing for me to rack up $3,000 or $4,000 a month. I kept waiting for the big sale, the

windfall that was going to pay all ___
Instead I'd sell a condo here and ___
another, and then nothing for a m___
agent left the office. He couldn't s___
his family going. There I was wit___
only two remained and one worke___

"One of my best friends in the b___
up my office and go to work for one___
but I was stubborn. I had worked ___
wasn't about to throw in the towel ___
was in denial, pure and simple. I w___
ity. You can't continue to go into de___
and expect to survive. But I didn't ___

What Becka's mind denied, her ___
having headaches and stomacha___
sleep more than an hour or two at a___
sick at one point that I collapsed in___
the supermarket. I was rushed to ___
later diagnosed with an ulcer. But e___
get my attention. The doctor gave m___
me to slow down and watch my diet.___
I had a business to run. Just give me___
out of here, I thought to myself."

Becka said she continued on th___
months, often working up to eighteen___
business got, the more money she sp___
the paper advertising her properties,___
credit cards. She leased a new car. S___
for her office, "all in an attempt to pro___
turn this around. I thought that if I ___
become prosperous again. I sound lik___
laughing.

"She was in business for herself to___
made a point of keeping up appearanc___
I was three, and she never remarried.___
to live with us so Mom could open her___
of her favorite slogans was 'You've got___
the part.' She believed that with all h___
ticed it too. She bought the best equ___
help, and leased space in the best par___

"I have a long way to go," said Becka, smiling meekly, "but now I'm going in the other direction, away from debt. And for the first time in years, I'm on my knees every morning, thanking God for this second chance."

Taking Inventory

Women who abuse credit cards answer "often" or "very often" to many of these statements:

1. I feel grown-up when I use credit cards.

2. I use credit cards for things I would not purchase with cash.

3. I pay only the minimum balance on my credit cards each month.

4. I use credit cards to charge emergency expenses—sick pets, flat tires, unexpected medical bills—because I don't have an emergency reserve.

5. I am close to or at the limit of all my credit cards.

6. I use one credit line to pay another.

7. I lose track of what I spend when I use credit cards.

8. I cannot imagine a life without credit cards.

6

Compulsive Gamblers

"**I**t only takes a dollar and a dream." So read the posters and television commercials for the New York state lottery. Similar enticements are on the rise throughout the country. In 1990 Americans bet $20.8 billion on the lottery in over thirty states. Gambling is now legal in forty-eight states—and expanding. As of June 1991, new casinos are open in Nevada, Maryland, New Jersey, and on Indian reservations.[1] As legalized gambling spreads, the number of problem gamblers also rises.

Dr. Sheila Blume of the South Oaks Hospital psychiatric treatment center in Amityville, New York, has studied female compulsive gamblers with Dr. Henry Lesieur, a professor of sociology at St. John's University in New York City. "Most are never recognized or treated,"[2] she said. "The sad fact is that we have elderly women playing bingo seven days a week with money they cannot afford to lose."

CLOSET GAMBLERS

Rose, a recovering gambler from Los Angeles, said that in her experience "there are a lot of closet female gamblers similar to those Dr. Blume and Dr. Lesieur have studied. Probably no one really knows how many there are," she said.

Rose believes the numbers are hazy, because gambling has always been a man's pursuit. "It's okay for men to go to the track, play poker, or shoot craps, but it's not okay for women," she said, rolling her eyes heavenward. "They should be at home raising the kids."

Blume and Lesieur agree that the numbers are inaccurate. Many women gamblers, unlike men who gamble, have high rates of other addictive behaviors and use gambling as a form of escape from their troubled lives. Fully 58 percent of the fifty female gamblers Lesieur interviewed had undergone psychotherapy before reaching Gamblers Anonymous—a support group modeled after Alcoholics Anonymous.

In many cases, Blume and Lesieur discovered that these women had not discussed their gambling addiction with their therapist. "When they had," Blume noted, "the gambling was often considered unimportant."

In truth, problem gambling among women is on the rise, possibly due to the increase of casino gambling, bingo, and state lotteries, forms of betting that are particularly attractive to women. Today women also have more discretionary money to spend, more independence as millions work outside their homes, and more leisure hours than their peers of a decade or two ago.

SUPPORT NEEDED

Dr. Lesieur claims that one in three compulsive gamblers is a woman. Unlike some researchers, he believes that "compulsive gambling is as treatable as alcoholism, yet fewer than one in ten women are in treatment."[3]

According to Lesieur, this is often the case "because they do not get the family support they need." Men, for example, are not as likely as women to attend Gam-Anon, the Twelve Step support program for spouses and families of gamblers. "Gambling has been perceived as a male-dominated activity."

On the other hand, it's unlikely that a support group for families of compulsive shoppers will ever form, he indicated, "because shopping is considered a female activity. In that case it would be the man who would attend such a meeting.

But since men, by and large, are not taught to be nurturers, they probably wouldn't organize or attend such a group."

This lack of support is one of the major problems female gamblers face. One woman I talked with said her husband confronted her after three years of her gambling and said, "I love you, but I'm not going to live like this anymore. Get help, or get out!" End of subject.

He did not look for a support system for himself. He did not blame himself for her gambling. He did not try to figure out how to save the relationship.

The reverse, however, is often true when the male in a relationship is the addict. The woman will usually accept at least some of the blame for the problem, remain with the abuser, and attend Gam-Anon, Al-Anon, or other support meetings in order to take care of herself and better understand the abuser.

ADVENTURE AND ESCAPE

Dr. Lesieur said his research "was prompted by the fact that there was so little being done about women and gambling. Most of the scientific journal research is based on men. Expressions such as 'big shot' and 'ego-oriented' make it clear that the data refers to males. In general, women don't exhibit these traits," he added.

However, as female gamblers have come forward, Lesieur has found "a more complete picture of the gambler, among women, because they are willing to talk about their process. Men don't talk that way." Female gamblers are also "clearly divisible," he said.

There is, first of all, what Lesieur calls the *adventure-seeker.* This woman responds to the high-risk action and adventure of gambling, which helps her feel like a different person. "Good girls" see gambling as a chance to be reckless, to go against the tide, to exercise power they were unable to experience during their earlier years.

Second, there is the *escape-seeker,* the woman who gambles to escape boredom, an unhappy home life, chronic pain, or loneliness. Female gamblers differ from males in that they generally do not make their first bet until they are adults.

Members of both groups are extremely lonely and troubled women. They also share some common characteristics with women who have other kinds of addictive behavior. Many suffer depression, low self-esteem, and in some cases come from a dysfunctional family.

Thirty-one of the fifty women Dr. Lesieur interviewed had problems with at least one parent, including sexual abuse, alcoholism, or mental illness. Many of these women "jumped from a problematic upbringing to a problematic marriage," he said.

CULTURAL STEREOTYPES

"Gambling is still very much stigmatized in our society," Lesieur added. "People tend to think in terms of two stereotypes when they think of women and gambling. There is the *irresponsible madonna,* who in the extreme, will leave her infant son in the car while she runs in to play bingo. And there's the *whore,* a woman who resorts to prostitution when in extreme debt. It's a known fact," said Lesieur, "that a lot of sexual activity goes on in the back rooms of the card parlors in Southern California."

These are the extremes, he admitted, but nevertheless, they are the images people have of women gamblers, similar to the stereotyped image people have of alcoholics as deadbeats staggering down the middle of the street or living in rags on skid row. The truth is there are millions of addicts of every kind who live in suburbia and work on Wall Street.

INVISIBLE ADDICTION

Gambling, unlike alcohol and drug addiction, however, has been something of an outsider in the recovery movement until a decade ago. Not until 1980 was compulsive gambling officially recognized as a psychological disorder by those in the mental health field. Dr. Lawrence J. Hatterer,[4] a Manhattan psychiatrist who has researched and written on the topic, calls compulsive gambling "a bit of a step-child in the addiction-treatment world."

Even the victims appear to be anything but down-and-out.

Many gamblers are high performers who excel in demanding professions such as law, sales, and medicine. Others are successful entrepreneurs, working hard to make the money they need to support their habit. Still others are singles, homemakers, and seniors.

EMERGING MOODS

The gambling process itself is a fascinating one. Tomas Martinez, author of *The Gambling Scene,*[5] describes this process in terms of five moods that emerge in individuals as their gambling increases. Many female gamblers can relate to his research.

Risk-taking

In the beginning the person must be willing to take risks. Once involved, she sees the risks as pleasurable. Wanda says she distinctly remembers the day she crossed the line from fear to pleasure. "I put my entire savings—$500—on a hand of blackjack—and I won. I felt so powerful in that moment that nothing and no one could touch me. It was a peak experience. I knew I'd be back."

Awareness of self in the here and now

Gamblers who experience this mood claim there is nothing like it. They are more aware of themselves and their personal power than they've ever been in their lives. They concentrate so totally on the immediate situation that no memory or thought of past or present can intrude. The pattern of betting and mastering the skills of the game builds a person's self-confidence to the point where she is certain she can handle herself in the moment. This mood also pulls her more deeply into the game.

"While I'm betting, I am filled with a sense of living I can't explain," said Betsy. "I know I'm alive. I *feel* the life pulsing through me. There is nothing like it. Nothing."

Fantasy

The more a woman gambles, the more she leaves present time. She becomes free to imagine herself living and participating at a level of life that has not seemed possible before. She begins to believe that she can be whatever she envisions. When she is away from the casino or card parlor she is reminded of her real life and the problems she faces. A return to gambling appears to be the only escape, so her drive to commit more funds and more time increases. Gambling is no longer a game. It becomes a measure of her identity.

Veda said that even after she had gambled away the $10,000 inheritance her grandmother had left her, she was still fantasizing about buying a Mercedes-Benz and going on a cruise to Alaska. "I just *knew* the answer was in the cards," she said. "The cards held the magic I couldn't find anyplace else. I believe it was then that I made a commitment to continue gambling until I acquired the lifestyle I felt I deserved."

Euphoria

This fourth mood, claims Martinez, is rare and short-lived. It occurs after cashing in on a long shot at the races or taking a large pot after a calculated bluff. It is the moment when a woman may feel closest to her real self—the part of her that knows power and poise and presence all at the same time.

Elena recalls a time when she bet on a horse, "because I liked his name. I didn't know anything about odds or performance at that time. But I won $2,000, and I remember the sense of euphoria that came over me. Most people would call it beginner's luck, but not me. I felt I had a knack for picking winners, and I could hardly wait to place my next bet."

Women who experience euphoria frequently pass from occasional to regular gambling at such times. Preserving their sense of well-being and self-esteem becomes more important than anything else. And the social support for their fantasized self feeds their hunger for more and more. Dealers, fellow players, and casino pit bosses prey upon such women. They have a vested interest in keeping a player feeling good about herself while gambling.

Mysticism

As a woman commits more and more time to gambling, her activities surrounding her betting become mystical, almost ritualistic. Dede, for example, said she had a "lucky" blouse that she wore for certain games on certain days. Alice bets specific denominations of money and never varies. Still others perform little rituals, such as walking around a casino three times before playing, or sitting on a particular stool or in a favorite chair.

Some individuals become very serious about this aspect of their gambling process. They use affirmations, visualizations, willpower, and other mind-control techniques in an effort to "find favor," as one woman put it, "with the gambling gods."

This mood stage, however, can have frightening and far-reaching spiritual consequences for the women involved, including dependence on witchcraft, psychic readings, and other forms of spiritual bondage in an effort to create a lucky streak.

PATHOLOGICAL GAMBLING

If the gambler chooses to continue the pleasure process, she will stay longer than she planned, become overly tired, and lose all sense of judgment and self-control. Then suddenly she feels the pain of losing more than she expected, is awakened abruptly from her dream state, and must face reality—at least for the moment. She is no longer free to fantasize. Her mood shifts to reality as she realizes she has no more money to play with, the game is over, the casino is closing, or a friend is dragging her away from the table.

She resolves not to play as long next time or lose as much. But the resolve is short-lived, as the hunger to make up for what she lost takes over. The only "cure" for the shifting mood is more gambling.

The losses escalate, however, because no system beats the house in the long run. The compulsive gambler continues to use whatever cash, credit card, credit line, or savings are available to acquire the money she needs to keep going. When those supplies run dry, however, she is at a crucial point. If she does not get help, she is likely to become frantic and turn to illegal means in a last-ditch effort to recover the losses—embezzling, stealing, writing bad checks, working credit card schemes, robbing children's college funds, and at the low ebb, prostitution.

At this point, the gambler is close to bottoming out. She can no longer shut out the pain of reality by gambling. In fact, gambling now creates as much or more pain than life itself, as Kitty, Carmen, and Brenda discovered in their terrifying dance with debt through compulsive gambling.

Just One of the Boys: Kitty's Story

Kitty said she's been a gambler since she was a kid. "I was the only seven-year-old girl flipping baseball cards against the garage wall for money," said the mother of two teenagers. "In high school I shot craps with the boys. And by the time I was in my twenties I was a regular in Vegas. In fact, my husband and I were married in Las Vegas," she said with a note of cynicism in her voice.

"When my son and daughter were little I'd escape the routine at home by hanging out at the card parlors in Gardena, California. I wasn't working at the time, so I took household money. I started winning, and that made it worse. I couldn't see the sense of paying the phone company or my Mastercard bill when I could use that $100 for poker—especially when I knew I could win."

Kitty said she stayed out all night, left her kids with friends and family, lied, cheated, and did whatever she had to do to keep the high going. "I gambled compulsively for three years," she said. "The funny thing is I still thought I was a good mother. At least I pretended I was. But the truth is when I was ready for a game, no one mattered—not my kids, not my husband, no one."

One December evening, before Christmas of 1979, Kitty said her husband finally drew the line. He confronted her head-on and told her that he and the kids loved her but they weren't going to take it anymore. "He told me about a group called Gamblers Anonymous, modeled after Alcoholics Anonymous. He said if I didn't go to a meeting and find out how to get help, I might as well pack up and leave—for good.

"But even that didn't stop me," she said. "Can you believe it? I told myself that I'd go to a meeting, lie low for a while, get him off my back, and then be back in the card rooms in a month or so."

But Kitty didn't go back in a month or a year or even five years. She's been free of compulsive gambling for nearly twelve years. "I attended my first GA meeting and hated it," she said. "I wasn't ready to change. But I had promised my husband I'd go for a month, so I did. And I kept coming back—because it started to work.

"In the opening readings of each GA meeting," said Kitty, "newcomers are invited to attend meetings for ninety days, and if they're not making progress after that, they can have their misery back," she said chuckling.

Kitty's children were nine and thirteen when she stopped gambling. "It took time, and a lot of patience, but we became a family again," she said with a sigh. "Actually, I was one of the lucky ones. We didn't have to sell our house or go bankrupt. But I did go to work to pay off the $15,000 debt I had run up on credit cards and everywhere else. I owed my brother money, my friends, anyone I could suck in."

Kitty talked about her birth family only briefly. "Both my parents were alcoholics," she said. "They died of the disease. To this day, I grieve over the fact that neither of them had the chance at recovery that I've had. I don't know if their patterns set off mine. I really don't know. I'm just going forward now—a day at a time—and thanking God for a second chance. For the first time in my life I know what it's like to be a real winner."

Born to Win: Carmen's Story

Forty-five-year-old Carmen owed more than $40,000 in gambling debts when she went into treatment at the Johns Hopkins University Compulsive Gambling Counseling Center near Baltimore, Maryland, during the early 1980s.

Carmen got her first taste of betting vicariously. Her grandfather, who lived with her family while she was growing up, went to the racetrack every Friday. "It was a ritual," she said. "Sometimes he won. Sometimes he lost. I don't remember anyone making much of it at the time. It was a hobby, like bowling or bridge. But when he did win, he'd share his winnings with my sister and brother and me. He might give us each only a dollar or two, but to me it was play money, money you didn't have to work for."

When Carmen was in college she worked part-time and went to school part-time, while still living at home. "I went to the track with my grandfather during that time, mostly because he was too old to drive by then, and he needed someone to stay with him. At first he placed bets for me, but after I turned eighteen, I began using my own money and making higher and higher bets.

"A month before I graduated from college, my grandfather suddenly passed away. I had no reason to go to the track anymore. But I did. I went for myself."

Before long everything in Carmen's life began to revolve around gambling. "I didn't date. I saw less and less of my girlfriends. I moved around a lot. I avoided my family. I never had a decent job. I waitressed. I drove a cab. I was a window washer for a time—anything to keep me going from one bet to the next. For a couple of months I was so broke I had to sleep in my car; yet I still believed it was just a matter of time until I'd win big."

Within two years after her grandfather's death, Carmen had gambled away the $10,000 inheritance he had left her. After running up credit lines, Carmen did whatever she could to shuffle funds. One scam she pulled off with some success was what she calls musical markets. "I'd move from one grocery market to another like a kid playing musical chairs," she said. "I'd pick up a quart of milk or a bag of apples, and pay for it with a worthless check for $10 over the purchase price. I'd pocket the change and run to the next market and do the same thing until I had enough to bet."

Some days, Carmen was so overwhelmed from chasing money, she barely had enough energy to get to the track. "At times I didn't know who I was or where I was going. It felt like a drunken stupor. But then I'd see the scoreboard and the odds for the next race, and I'd get into it again. I wouldn't be satisfied until I gambled every penny I had. I figured it wasn't my money anyway, so what difference did it make?"

Carmen looked away for a moment, then continued. "I was a

pretty tough cookie in those days. Sometimes I can't believe it was really me. When I think of my sweet grandpa I could cry. He never meant for things to turn out this way. He was just having fun. I made it a way of life."

Carmen remembers with gratitude the first few weeks at the center. "The counselors put all the patients through some eighty hours of group and individual therapy," she said, "to help us see that we were responsible for the condition we were in and also to see that we had the power to turn it around."

Counselors at the center spend the first two weeks breaking through ingrained defenses and modeling effective ways of dealing with others. "I was a loner, and I lied to myself and everyone else," said Carmen. "I didn't want to take responsibility for myself. I wanted someone—anyone—to come along and bail me out. But it doesn't work that way. Women who had rescuers shared in group that the more help they had, the more they gambled. They didn't get well until the pain of pretending was worse than the pain of treatment."

Carmen also made a list of all her gambling debts during the first two weeks—a requirement for all patients. She couldn't imagine how she'd ever pay them off, but she said she felt better seeing them in black and white. It was a good reality check, as they say."

Carmen is out of treatment now and finished with the two years of outpatient visits following her release in 1983. She now lives in Los Angeles where she attends regular meetings of Gamblers Anonymous.

She works as a sales rep for a pharmaceutical company, making $38,000 a year. She has paid off two credit lines totaling $20,000 and expects to be totally solvent within the next three to five years, based on a repayment plan she has worked out with her sponsor in GA.

Carmen is also involved in a support group for Christian women led by a counselor in her church. Through these sessions she has learned that people are one of her greatest assets. "I have spent too much of my life running," she said. "Now I have a place to come where I can be heard and understood and loved. And I am beginning to trust God for the first time in my life."

Gambling Away Grief: Brenda's Story

Brenda, unlike Kitty and Carmen, had a protected child-hood. "I was an only child," she said, "so I lived in an adult world a lot of the time. My parents were older—they had me in their early forties, after thinking they'd never have a child. When I arrived they devoted themselves to me, took me on fabulous vacations, and spent time on things I was interested in. They even bought me a horse when I was in junior high."

During high school, Brenda's dad died suddenly of a heart attack, and she and her mother bonded even more tightly. "We did everything together," said Brenda. "My mother was a very special person, bright, pretty, full of life. People who knew her tell me I'm like her in all the right ways. I like to think that's true. I loved her very much."

Brenda did not marry. "I didn't choose to remain single," she said. "It just worked out that way. I stayed on with my mother, and when she got older, we sold our family home and bought a two-bedroom condo. It was easier for her and for me too, since I owned a small stationery store and had little time to take care of a large house."

But a year after they moved, Brenda's mother was killed instantly in an automobile accident, and Brenda's entire life changed in that moment.

"Following her death, I was at a total loss," she said. "The purpose for my life seemed to have died with her. I lost interest in my business, even though I had done extremely well, grossing $350,000 the year before my mother died."

Brenda had other problems adjusting to life on her own. "I realized that first year how much I had depended on my parents for nurturing and companionship," she said. "Usually it's the other way around. The elderly parent depends on the adult child. But my parents and I were like the three muske-teers. We did everything together. And when it was just Mom and me, the bond was intensified."

Brenda had few close friends, but one greeting card sales rep she had become friendly with over the course of their business dealings seemed especially sympathetic. "She urged me to get away from the shop, to meet some new people, and to have fun. She invited me to drive to Atlantic City with her for a weekend. She had heard about the casinos and wanted to see what they were like. I was curious, so in a moment of weakness, I said yes, even though I was still grieving the loss of my mother."

Brenda's friend Judy got a roll of quarters and headed for the slot machines. Brenda went to the blackjack table. "I had played the game for fun at the home of friends, so I was less intimidated by this game than the crap table. The machines seemed like a waste of time to me." Before the night was over, Judy agreed. She had lost $20 and decided gambling wasn't for her. "In fact, she didn't want to stay the full weekend," said Brenda, "so we called it quits and came home Saturday afternoon."

But unlike Judy, Brenda thought it was great fun. For the first time in months she had laughed and talked with people, and the dealer smiled and encouraged her. "I felt special," said Brenda, "even though I lost $75. I could afford to lose it, so it didn't upset me. In fact, I chalked it up to entertainment expenses. I'd spend that much on a theater ticket in New York, so I didn't think it was a big deal."

Brenda returned the next weekend and the next. Then before long she couldn't wait for the weekends. She began closing her shop early during the week and going up two or three nights in a row. "At first I pretty much broke even. I didn't worry about being up or down a couple of hundred dollars. It seemed like an inexpensive way to have fun. Besides, I hadn't felt so youthful or so well in years.

"It was another world to me. I'd put on a pretty dress, fix my hair, walk through the casino, and feel like somebody. I could escape the routine of my shop for a few hours and forget my grief.

"I even got attached to a certain seat at a particular table," said Brenda, flashing her deep brown eyes. "It felt like mine. I was sure the dealer had saved it for me till I could come back —which, of course, I did, again and again, until I went through the $50,000 my mother left me after she died. But still my shop was thriving. I had hired two girls to take over while I was away, and they did such a good job of running the place I hardly gave it a thought."

Brenda's confidence began to soar and so did her betting. "Gradually I moved my bets from $200 to $500 in a single evening. I could see that my losses had far exceeded my winnings, but I felt certain I'd win it all back next time, and besides, I told myself, this was my entertainment. Other people had expensive cars or a boat or skiing equipment. I spent a little on gambling. What was the harm?"

Within six months Brenda was a regular four and five nights a week. The pit bosses and dealers knew her by name. She was offered a line of credit and even qualified for transportation in a chauffeur-driven limousine.

"I was now part of the club—a 'high roller' as they are called. I took out two lines of credit at two different casinos for $50,000 each. But even that wasn't enough. I tapped my savings and began withdrawing money from my business. Eventually, I had to let one of my employees go because I couldn't pay her regularly."

Brenda saw an article about gambling in an issue of *Parade* magazine and it sent a chill down her spine. "But I was in such denial at that time," she said, "that I brushed it off, telling myself I was different. I was a social gambler, not a problem gambler."

By the end of the first year Brenda was a wreck. She never got enough sleep, she didn't eat appropriately, and she stopped calling friends. "All I could think of was blackjack. Sometimes I'd wake up in the middle of the night in a cold sweat, wishing the hours away so I could get back to the table and make up for all I'd lost."

The end was in sight—though Brenda did not yet know it. She went to her bank one morning about two months into her second year, to withdraw funds for the weekend. She was shocked to find out that she was down to $125. "I hadn't looked at my bank statement in months," she said. "I just assumed there'd always be plenty. There always had been. The year before I had a balance of $75,000."

Brenda said she panicked, not because there was so little money, but because it meant she couldn't go to Atlantic City that weekend. She couldn't imagine staying home. She hadn't been alone in her house for more than a couple of hours at a time in over a year.

"It was then that I thought about cashing in one of my retirement accounts. It was all I had left. I told myself it was my only solution. I actually considered starting the process that very afternoon. The only problem was that I wouldn't be able to get the money in my hands for several days, perhaps weeks. Then there was the penalty for early withdrawal, tax consequences, and so on. I didn't mind that so much except for the time it would take. I begrudged anything that took me away from the tables."

Then Brenda remembered two savings bonds her mother had bought for her years ago when she graduated from college. She had completely forgotten about them until that moment.

She took them out of her safety deposit box, cashed them in, and drove to the casino that night, arriving about 10:00. Within two hours she had parlayed the $5,000 into $20,000. "I was on such a high that I told myself I couldn't possibly quit."

Brenda grabbed a few hours sleep, then returned to the tables first thing Saturday morning. By noon she had lost the $20,000 and an additional $5,000 extended on her credit line at the casino.

"I got into my car that afternoon," she said, "and considered driving off a cliff." The limousine, the free meals, the posh hotel rooms were suddenly history. Brenda was a woman deeply in debt. She owed two casinos $105,000, and she had drained her own savings and business accounts of nearly $200,000. The only thing she had left was her condominium. Her mortgage payment was the one bill she had faithfully paid.

"My shop went bankrupt within two months. I couldn't pay the rent, I had lost my customer base, and my one remaining employee quit. I couldn't pay her. I had never been so low in my life. I considered taking an overdose of sleeping pills, slashing my wrists, anything to end the excruciating pain. And to make matters worse, I kept seeing my mother's face. I couldn't even get out of bed for three days."

On the fourth day, Brenda's friend Judy called and said she had heard Brenda had gone out of business. "Judy had changed companies, so we lost touch for a number of months," said Brenda. "Little wonder! I didn't answer phone calls or letters. I wasn't home long enough to know what was going on. I broke down at the sound of her voice—thinking back to that first fateful weekend when we had driven to Atlantic City together. I told her the whole story. She came over that night and brought some literature she had gotten from a friend who had been in treatment for compulsive gambling. That was the first step of my long road back.

"Like thousands of others, I'm in Gamblers Anonymous now, and I'm trying to live one day at a time. But it's hard. I actually miss the good times—or what seemed like good times. But there's no going back. I know that. I also know that if I had continued on, I'd be on the street today—a bag lady.

"I came this close," she said, holding her right forefinger just above her thumb, "to losing my condo—the only security I had left. I'm working at a department store now, and I've made up a repayment plan with the help of someone in GA. I call it my hundred-year plan," she said, laughing, "because it feels like it'll take forever to pay it back. But I can't worry about that now. I have to make the commitment—it's part of my recovery. Besides, now I have someone to lean on who's bigger than me: Jesus Christ. I became a Christian through my sponsor in GA," she said, smiling. "One of my favorite passages in Scripture is from the book of Joel: 'I will restore to you the years that the swarming locust has eaten.' I am clinging to that promise and trusting that God will do for me what I can't do for myself" (2:25).

Taking Inventory

Women who are compulsive gamblers answer "often" or "very often" to many of these statements:

1. I gamble with money I cannot afford to lose.

2. I am preoccupied with winning and/or recouping my losses.

3. I feel restless when I am not gambling or planning a gambling trip.

4. I find myself increasing my bets in order to experience greater excitement.

5. I gamble to escape my troubled life.

6. I enjoy the status and attention I receive while gambling.

7. I neglect my family, community, social, and recreational activities in favor of gambling.

8. I continue to gamble despite my rising debts.

9. I am secretive about my gambling and the money I use for betting.

10. I have borrowed, stolen, or used household or business funds for my gambling.

11. I cannot stop gambling, despite repeated efforts to try.

12. I would rather gamble than do anything else.

7

Debting Enablers

Many women in debt did not get there by spending or charging or shopping or gambling. They got there by *enabling* someone else—husband, parent, child, close friend, or associate—to go into or remain in debt. Typically, a debting enabler, like any other enabler, is a woman whose tolerance for emotional and physical pain is inordinately high. She generally suffers from low self-esteem and has trouble confronting others about emotionally charged issues.

Dianne was a debting enabler. So was Anne Marie, and so was I. I use the past tense because all three of us have stopped this behavior. We have stopped doing for others what they can do for themselves. We have stopped trusting others to make choices for us. And we have stopped the cover-ups, the lying, the controlling, and the enmeshment that made us victims of debt.

But the power to make these changes did not come overnight. Nor did the wisdom nor the insight. It was a slow and steady process, and for all three of us it was a life-changing, spiritual experience. But this is not unique to us. This experience is available to any woman who truly desires to release herself from this self-made prison.

Debt enabling is a particularly insidious and subtle form of money dysfunction. Those of us who enable are often oblivious to our part in the debting process. We are often as quick to rescue as we are to blame, and as eager to deny our part as we are to defend ourselves when pushed too far.

In the following pages, you will read Dianne's story, Anne Marie's story, and finally, my own. Each story is unique to the individual, yet similar in many ways.

A Bear Named Hope: Dianne's Story

"Having money was a high priority in my family when I was growing up," said Dianne, a soft-spoken woman with a kind face and a warm presence. "Although we were always on the verge of spending to the limit, our limit was high. My father was a chief executive with United States Steel, and we enjoyed the benefits of his status. We had a Cadillac and a private plane and plenty of everything."

Dianne's parents also set a high priority on women not working. It was assumed that Dianne and her sister would marry so they would be taken care of. "A nice house, cute kids, and possessions would equal happiness," she added.

Despite the appearances, however, Dianne's family lived with "an elaborate system of cover-ups." Her father was an alcoholic, and her mother covered up for him. When he passed out from drinking, she took him to a hotel, and the personnel there put him to bed until he could return home sober. "I never once saw him drunk," said Dianne. "In fact, I did not even know my father was an alcoholic until after I was married."

During Dianne's childhood her mother blamed her father's erratic behavior and bad temper on the kids or on his "stressful and important job." They grew up believing their father's high earning power meant that he loved them. Therefore, it was their job to keep him from getting upset so he could continue to work and provide for them.

"I was given so much money over the years," said Dianne, "that by the time I went to college, I bought bonds with some of it. I couldn't spend it all. I *always* had an excess," she added.

Dianne married with the same expectation she had grown up with—her husband would take care of her so she wouldn't have to work.

"My husband was a doctor, graduated from an Ivy League school, and made a lot of money," she said. "But he also lied, cheated, had numerous affairs, and threatened suicide throughout our nearly thirty years of married life. I chose someone who turned out to be mean and cruel," she said, pondering her words for a moment.

Over their years together, Dianne did as her mother had done. "Whenever there was a problem, I assumed I was at fault. I told myself that I must have done something wrong to bring on so much trouble. So I did whatever I could to keep peace, to keep the facade going."

Then Dianne's husband began to tighten his control on their money. He stopped giving her what she needed for the kids' clothing and food and household items. "That's when I started using credit cards," she said, "to keep up appearances. In four years I charged $30,000. One card alone had an $18,000 limit." Dianne paid the bills so her husband was not aware of the mounting debt. "I opened a post office box so the bills wouldn't come to our home address," she said.

But the stress in her home escalated. Her husband was sexually and physically abusive, threatened her life, and more than once tried to strangle her.

"For years, I kept my car packed, ready to leave on a moment's notice," she said. "The four kids had their suitcases ready too. They kept them under their beds. The older ones knew that when I gave the signal, they were to pick up the younger ones, grab their suitcases, and meet me in the car."

Despite all this turmoil, however, Dianne continued to enable her husband's behavior as her mother had done with her father. "I was in total denial," she said. One day when she was out of the house, her husband tried to strangle their middle daughter.

Their oldest daughter, completely shaken by this event, confided in a counselor at her high school. She came home that day and confronted her mother. "She told me there was something very wrong with our family. But I wasn't ready, even then, to accept it. I told her and the counselor that we were fine. We were a normal family, and we didn't need help."

But the kids didn't give up. They heard about Al-Ateen, a Twelve Step support program for teens with an alcoholic parent, and attended a meeting on their own. Afterward the children confronted her. "My son and three daughters cornered me one night in a booth at a restaurant and told me they wanted me to go to an Al-Anon meeting. I broke down and cried, and promised I'd go."

After listening to others share at the meeting, Dianne knew she had a problem. It was that night that she also found out about Debtors Anonymous. "I got into that program right away. I knew I was ready to get well. I cut up my credit cards, made a list of all my debts, and contacted my creditors."

Dianne knew the debts were hers, but she also knew they had come about because of years of enabling her husband to remain in debt to his family. She had lied, kept secrets, and protected their appearance in order to save her family and the lifestyle they had built.

Dianne also participated in a special meeting of Debtors Anonymous, called a Pressure Group, designed to take the pressure off, as one member shares with two other members her financial picture—debts, goals, and a plan for restitution. A Pressure Group meeting can also be a place to build a realistic spending plan that includes savings as well as debt repayment.

"I learned from the two people who helped me that secrets were my biggest problem," said Dianne. "They encouraged me to tell my husband what I had done, to take responsibility for these debts, and to talk with him about a reasonable budget for our family."

Her next step was a meeting with her husband's psychiatrist. She told him what she wanted to accomplish, and he helped her arrange an intervention—a meeting where she could confront her husband with other people in the room to support her. When they met, she showed her husband her debts and her plan for repaying them by going to work. "His response was clear and direct. 'I don't want to be in this marriage.'"

She knew she could not stay in their home with him and risk more violence to the children, so she went to a shelter for battered women until her husband moved out. Since then they have filed for divorce, sold their house, and paid off the debt. Dianne now lives with her grown children in another location. "Even though my world was falling apart, I had to keep trusting that the future would be good, because it would be based on honesty."

Today Dianne is working as a nurse and studying for her graduate degree. "It feels great to get a paycheck," she said. "It has changed my life. Now I really feel good about myself." She knows she can take care of herself and her family. "All four of my kids are in private counseling, and we are gradually rebuilding our family of five—instead of six—through family therapy."

Dianne is also aware of God's work in her life in even the simplest of things. For example, one day she bought herself a teddy bear—a treat for the little girl within her. But she couldn't think of a name right away. Then one evening, during a prayer meeting at her mother's home, the leader talked about the significance and meaning of names throughout the Bible.

"I still hadn't named my bear," she said, smiling. "So I was interested in what he was saying. That night I had a dream and in it I felt God was encouraging me in my life. He told me that the support systems in my life represented *love,* that my job is to have *faith,* and to hold on to *hope.* I knew in that moment what I'd name my bear—Hope. Now whenever I look at him or hold him, I am reminded of that message." Since then Dianne has given bears to her mother, her sisters, and each of her children.

The Untouchables: Anne Marie's Story

"My dad was a career officer in the military," said Anne Marie, an attractive thirty-eight-year-old therapist with warm eyes and deep dimples. "He liked the stable income and the excitement of being a pilot." Anne Marie is the oldest of five children, and she feels that both her parents set a good example when it came to money. "They always saved for cars, made wise investments, and made money on every house they bought. But for some reason, I didn't pick up their habits."

She does see, however, how she has patterned some of her behavior after her mother. "She was the soother, the more upbeat person in the marriage. My dad was charismatic, but he was also very mercurial. He had a darker side—perhaps as a result of his own father, who committed suicide when my dad was sixteen. When his dark moods would come up in different ways, I watched my mother enable his feelings. She has largely outgrown that today, but I remember it as a child."

Anne Marie sees that same pattern in her relationship with her husband, Sidney. "That's how we hook up. I fell in love with someone who is crazy around money and for several years I enabled him to stay that way. Money has always been an *untouchable* subject between us.

"I learned that trying to change people definitely doesn't work. So when I married Sidney I didn't even try. At first we had plenty of money. We were both working, and so we pretty much did our own thing.

"For example, I remember a time when we were just getting acquainted. He lost $70 one night playing poker. I think he felt bad about it. So to compensate, the next day he bought me a stuffed animal for $100."

But all that changed when their first child was born. "I couldn't work as much, so naturally our income dropped. We went into debt about $1,000 a month for two years."

Anne Marie was so involved with her therapy practice and her baby daughter that she let Sidney handle their finances. "Somehow he kept it going in his head. He began staggering the payments until it became overwhelming." That's when Anne Marie started looking for help. She found out about Debtors Anonymous and attended her first meeting.

After two months, she and her husband scheduled a Pressure Group. "The man and woman who did our Pressure Group suggested that we set *emotional* as well as *task* goals, and to this day that has been one of the most effective tools we use."

Anne Marie and Sidney now meet with each other once or twice a week to deal with money. "Before we get into the money issues, however, first we talk about how we want to *feel* during the meeting." They both said that feeling good about themselves helps them talk about the untouchable subject in a more sane and balanced way.

"For me, having to tell our creditors that they'd have to wait, not being able to pay off everything at once, was the most shameful thing on earth for me." But doing it was an important step in her recovery.

As a child Anne Marie had "math phobia," and that left her with the idea that she couldn't deal with financial matters. "But it's not true. I've changed by seeing that I actually know more about money conceptually than Sidney does. I've given up the notion that he understands it just because he's a man and six years older than I am. I've also gotten more forceful." Anne Marie is now teaching her husband what she knows. "I never used to speak up. Now I do, and he's listening." And he "has been humbled and changed since he started the DA program. He's now willing to keep track of all his expenses, and he no longer uses credit cards."

They are seeing changes for the better in their therapy practice as well. "I'm a lot clearer now about my clients' fees and insurance billing. I'm also seeing that I relate better to couples who have problems with debt. I listen more effectively, and I can help them discover how to talk about the untouchable topics in their relationships."

For Anne Marie and Sidney, Debtors Anonymous has provided the practical tools that have allowed them to turn around their destructive patterns with money. "It's a behavioral experience," she said, "a very nuts-and-bolts approach that works."

She also believes in tackling a problem from more than one angle. "Any two types of therapy are better than one. The more ways you can look at a problem, the more success you'll have at solving it. I like a combination of individual therapy, group therapy when appropriate, and a Twelve Step program." Anne Marie finds that Debtors Anonymous and other similar programs bring a spiritual dimension to the healing process, which is not always available in private therapy.

At this stage of their recovery, Anne Marie and Sidney now have a savings account that is too large to leave in a straight passbook account. By using the tools of Debtors Anonymous they have learned to take care of themselves, even as they take care of their debts. They save 10 percent of their earnings, send 20 percent to their creditors and live on 70 percent. And at the time we talked they were in the process of finding investment vehicles for their excess funds, and were passing on to their clients and others the hands-on approach they follow in dealing with a subject that was once untouchable.

The Case That Never Happened: My Story

My first husband came from a family with a modest income. There were few luxuries, but their needs were always met. In contrast, I had come from a prosperous home where we had everything we needed and wanted. I never felt financially deprived. I liked nice things, and I was used to them. But because I had not known material lack, I was less driven to accumulate than my husband appeared to be.

In fact, over the years of our marriage, I remember being torn between his desire to acquire and my fear of debt. But I loved him, and I enjoyed the dreams we shared. One day he'd be a famous attorney, and we'd have a wonderful house and new cars, and we'd take fabulous vacations—the kind my parents had taken me on when I was a child. I wanted that same life for my children, and I had absolute faith and trust that if anyone could provide these things it would be my husband, whom I adored.

And so we bought our first house before we could comfortably afford the payments; we traded in good cars for new cars; we joined a private tennis and swim club when the public court and pool would have been just fine; and we bought our second house, tripling our monthly payments, during a crucial time in both our family life and his law practice.

We had barely enough money to squeak through the front door when escrow closed, and we had no cushion for emergencies. I was a wreck on moving day, but at the same time I was in love with my new dream house and with my husband, whom I knew I could count on to pull it off.

Every time a scary thought came up, I pushed it away. It was clear to both of us that I was the one with the problem. He wasn't worried. Why should I be? I started giving myself pep talks. I needed more faith. I needed to stand by my husband and support him. Keep his spirits up so he could work.

But I had a profound sense of despair amid the affluence around me. I felt that we were living a lie. Whenever we needed or wanted something, we hopped on the merry-go-round of debt once again, certain that *this* ride would be our last. That "big" legal case was just around the corner. Soon we would be solvent for good.

But the longer we stayed on the whirling carousel, the faster it went, round and round until I had all I could do just to hang on. Something was terribly wrong. I felt it. I knew it. But I was powerless to change it.

Money held us hostage on every front. We thought about it, stewed over it, chased it, spent it before we earned it, borrowed, charged, borrowed, and charged some more. Every time we received a cash gift or a settlement from a legal case, the money was accounted for before we even deposited it. I began to see my life through the eyes of money. Our debts were so far ahead of us that lack continually licked at our heels.

But my husband knew how to soothe me. "It's really better to live on other people's money," he said. "We can have what we want now, while we're young, while I'm building my practice. Then we'll be able to pay it all off with one check." And besides, there were great tax benefits. We could deduct the interest on our credit purchases, and we were building our TRW rating!

He was convincing. He was out in the world. He was a lawyer. I was a stay-at-home mom. What did I know? My mother had left such matters to my dad. Why couldn't I do the same with my husband?

I had to try harder—that was it. Be more patient, believe more fully, and remain loyal. I'd be all right for another six months or a year, and then it would start all over again—the sick feeling in the pit of my stomach, the restless nights, the lack of communication between us, his need to borrow one last time, and my signing yet another loan.

As my husband debted, I attempted to bring some order and control to our home life. I paid all the bills, balanced the checkbook, and carefully planned our expenses for food and clothing and vacations and car maintenance. I loved telling him how prudent and careful I had been, hoping to be acknowledged for my good work, hoping that he'd appreciate my support. He didn't acknowledge me. He didn't notice me. I had become so dependable that he didn't even have to think about me. I carried the weight of his disease for him. I suffered the stomach pains, the headaches, the fear, and terror. I was his full-time enabler. I freed him to practice his addiction big time.

And he didn't waste a minute. He borrowed, purchased, in-

1, until every dollar I had accumulated from my divorce
ment was gone.

certainly wasn't lazy. I believe he really tried. But, like
is illness around money was rooted deep within his
The natural realm did not hold the answer we were
g, but we didn't know then.

the time Charles and I had been married five years, we
one through my entire savings, and at one point we'd
reach out to our church to make our rent payments.
concept of living within one's income or paying cash
car or gas or clothes or dinner was totally outside my
y. The *idea* of living a solvent life appealed to me, but I
n't imagine how one could make it happen.

this time I was nearly insane with fear. There I was at
five years of age, practically broke, married a second
to the first man I had ever connected with in ways that
mattered to me. Yet the same pattern was emerging.
I was enabling someone who abused money.

afternoon over lunch I poured out my story to a friend,
he recommended a book, *Women Who Love Too Much* by
Norwood.[2] I read it in two sittings. It was as though she
ritten it just for me. Everything began to make sense. I
woman who loved too much—a woman who made men
ibstance of choice. When I reached the part of the book
ocused on steps for recovery, I stopped after reading the
ne: *Go for help.*[3]

d. I called a friend who had organized a Twelve Step
ort group at our church and attended my first meeting,
ng, crying, and fearful of what lay ahead. I had been in
py years before, so I knew that recovery requires time
ard work. I honestly didn't know if I was up to it. The
of repeating a pattern I'd sworn I would never practice
nearly overwhelmed me.

e again I was powerless over my life. I attended meet-
egularly, but insight and change were slow to come. I
reading books, listening to tapes, and attending work-
on prayer and healing. I began to feel different inside,
igh circumstances on the outside weren't much better.
is time my husband was in real estate, and when that
try began to crumble all around us, we finally hit bot-

vested, and spent without consulting me in any way. He
bought a private airplane, a car telephone, property in North-
ern California, a part of a ranch in Southern California, a new
car, and new office decor without so much as a nod in my
direction.

When I suggested that we purchase government bonds as a
college fund for our three children, he smiled at my naivete.
"By then I'll be able to pay cash for the whole thing," he said
with customary confidence. That "big" case would surely
come to pass before Julie, our oldest, was ready to enter
UCLA—some ten years in the future.

As I write about these events now, nearly two decades later,
I am struck by the level of denial and pain I lived through
during those years—pain so deep and so far-reaching that the
only way I could survive was to find a way to make his actions
acceptable. I did just that. It was my next project. I enabled
my husband to keep us on the edge financially, because I
didn't know how to separate my identity from his.

But coursing through me at a deeper level were the troubled
waters of fear, insecurity, enmeshment, and sheer terror of
there not being enough. I did not have words for my emotions
in those years. I operated on automatic for most of that marriage. It was impossible for me to halt the many loans and
debts we continued to acquire.

As I watched our credit card debt reach the limit, or another
loan come through to pay off the old loans, I trusted, yet
again, that all we needed was a little more time—for his practice to escalate, for the orthodontia to be paid off, for car
payments to cease, for me to find a way to earn.

For a while I tutored students in reading and math after
school and during the summer for $7 an hour. I saved every
penny I earned for vacations and extras, but soon even that
was needed to keep us afloat.

I became overwhelmed at what little difference it made. I
would gather my courage, approach my husband, and tell him
of my fear. He would calm me down temporarily with the
promise of the "big case that will wipe out everything we
owe." How I wanted to believe him!

By the mid-seventies, I was so emotionally ill that I didn't
know where to turn. I didn't feel nourished by the Catholic
church we were attending, so we stopped going to church. I

realized I didn't know how to pray, and by then God seemed like a stranger—if indeed He even existed. I was in turmoil twenty-four hours a day; yet I kept going, sure that things would get better if I just tried a little harder.

I distracted myself by taking a couple of correspondence courses in writing for publication. I loved writing. I believed I had found my niche. Then I noticed my depression begin to lift as I started selling a few articles to local newspapers and small magazines. The first year I made $400, the next year $1,000. Doing something creative for myself helped me regain some sense of self-worth and control. But as I look back now I see that my entire focus was on amassing money.

I became driven to earn. Whenever an opportunity to write came up I rarely considered anything but the financial end of it. How much could I make to help offset our mounting debt? I had taken on the problem. Now I felt it was my job to figure out a solution.

I see now that I was truly a woman in debt. Even though I was opposed to credit of any kind, I was as much a participant as an accomplice to murder. I enabled my husband to keep us on the merry-go-round of debt for nearly twenty years. No matter how sick and crazy it made me, no matter how much damage it laid down in the lives of our children, I didn't stop it.

I honestly didn't know how to do it any other way. If I had known differently, I would have done differently. In December 1979 we were divorced. He had met someone two years before whom he claimed loved him exactly the way he was. As far as I can tell, from the minute she walked into his life, he never looked back.

I came out of that marriage with half the assets from our house and half the debts—which were considerable. Still, I had close to $100,000. I was certain it would last me the rest of my life if I invested it wisely. But I was to engage in the dance of debt again—this time with a new partner—the man I am now married to.

Charles and I met within a year after my husband and I filed for divorce. We fell in love, moved in together, then parted when I became a Christian in December 1982. We reunited a couple of months later when he too made a commitment to Jesus Christ. We married the following month, April 1983.

Charles was out of work and in debt when I m when I married him, but I didn't look at that. All I responsive, caring person who adored me. I had no he would work hard, as soon as he found the righ pay back everyone he owed. At the time I had no i was to become his next creditor.

Once again I took up the familiar role of cheerleade advisor, and longsuffering partner. And after we were I added two new roles: prayer warrior and Christian w Christ in our corner how could we go wrong!

What I didn't know at the time was that becoming tian does not change debting into solvency overnight. Buhler often says, "If you were a bad cook before you l a Christian, coming to Christ doesn't turn you into cook. You're still a bad cook—who happens to be a tian."[1] Christianity is not magic. God will work in us sup urally, but he doesn't skip over the process.

I had a little more financial savvy this time, but not en At the beginning of our relationship we kept our finances arate, since he was in debt and I wasn't. But as soon as we married, I assumed the same role I'd had in my first marr

Even though I was working as a writer and language consultant and doing very well, I depended on him emc ally to the point of sickness. I felt that it was my job to " him—no matter what it cost me. While he recovered fro ing a job, I took on extra work. While he worked as a manager at a gas station and then a clerk at a dry cle and then a stock room supervisor at a cellular phon pany, I continued to keep our lifestyle afloat.

We still ate out frequently, went to movies, had thea concert tickets, and took short vacations—*on me!* The I didn't want to give up the life I had been leading, and would be selfish to do these things without him. Mea we didn't communicate about money—except for my crying jags and verbal harangues when I would cor emotionally.

Meanwhile, I continued to write checks each m supplement his income, to pay unexpected bills as h hard to get something going. At first it was just a hundred dollars a month, but then the amount incr fore long I was writing checks for several thousand

In 1988, he lost $40,000 in real estate commissions from cancelled escrows. The following year, with over $5,000 due in taxes and bills up to our eyebrows, we filed for bankruptcy. It was one of the most humiliating experiences of my life.

It wasn't until much later that I realized how invested I was in money. I had made it a power greater than myself. I had depended on money and men instead of depending on God. What a painful and shame-filled discovery that was.

Over the following months I was led to a support group for people who have problems with money. Did I have problems! I needed every bit of support the group had to offer. I returned week after week. Gradually, as God gave me the eyes to see and the ears to hear, I began to make sense of what had been half a lifetime of nonsense. I began to see that I was the problem—not my first husband and not my second one. They had trouble with money, to be sure. But the problems I had regarding their debting had to do with *me*—my self-esteem, my fear of being left alone, of being abandoned, of growing up and taking full responsibility for my life, financially and in every other way.

Instead I invested in my husbands, both emotionally and financially, to the extent that I had nothing left for myself, for my business, for my children, for vacations, for the recovery I needed and deserved.

I discovered through therapy and by participating in support groups, that I enabled others so I wouldn't have to look at myself, so I wouldn't end up alone.

I specifically invested in my second husband's business ventures so that he could do for me what I was terrified of doing for myself. I know better now. We both do. We no longer depend on each other for financial provision. Each morning, we ask God for guidance in all our affairs. We have a long way to go, but now we know who our true source is—and we go to Him together each morning.

Taking Inventory

Women who are debting enablers answer "often" or "very often" to many of these statements:

1. I do for others with money what they can and should do for themselves.

2. I take responsibility for the debts of others—especially family members or other significant people in my life.

3. I assist others financially without considering the consequences to myself.

4. I feel guilty about having money when others don't have enough.

5. I have few or no boundaries around loaning or giving away money.

6. I spend money freely on others while my own needs go unmet.

7. I make excuses for my spouse, adult children, or close friends who do not take financial responsibility for their lives.

8. I compulsively loan or give away money despite repeated attempts to stop.

9. I allow my husband, boyfriend, parents, or adult children to keep me in debt with their irresponsible spending patterns.

10. I co-sign for loans that I am uncomfortable with.

8

Under-earners

Under-earning is a painful and chronic condition for many women in debt. Those who have shared this process with me say it has left them with a profound sense of anger, shame, even despair of ever turning it around. Several said they find themselves settling for or remaining in jobs that are clearly beneath their level of education, below their hopes and desires, and behind other women of similar training and talent because they can't envision anything better. Then, as they continue working for low or minimum wages, they resort to abusing credit when they can't pay their bills.

UNDER-EARNING: A LIFESTYLE

For many women in debt, under-earning has become a way of life. Some, like Liz, don't fully understand why or how they got into this predicament. "I started working for Arby's when I was in high school, and here I am ten years later—in the same place. I'm the location manager now, so that's a step up," she said, laughing with embarrassment. "But still, when I look at the people I graduated with, this is a joke. I mean, come on—still slinging fast food, and I'm nearly thirty years old."

Liz admits, however, that she feels comfortable because she knows she can do the job, management likes her, and it's a familiar environment. "I've received numerous employee awards. Maybe that's what keeps me going." Liz feels that by now she should be in an upper management position or at least moving in that direction, but the thought of it scares her.

"I tell myself I don't need much money. The truth is I have nothing outside my paycheck. I live in a rented room and drive an old car. I have no savings to speak of and about $3,000 in credit card debt."

Other women who under-earn deliberately chose the job they're in because they didn't have higher goals, considered the work temporary, or didn't have any reality about what they truly needed. "I took a part-time job as a seamstress when my kids were young, because I could do some of the work at home," said Raylene. "I had sewn for myself and my kids, so I figured I could do it. Now that I'm divorced I need more money, but I'm too scared. I'm not sure I could do anything else."

She paused for a moment, then added, "When I talk like that I hear my ex-husband's voice, telling me I'd never be able to make it without him. I believed him—apparently I still do. I keep myself in this low-paying job, still dependent on the small alimony check he sends once a month. But that won't be there forever."

Many women who under-earn say they feel guilty when they even consider improving their lot. To some it's equivalent to an act of treason against their families—especially families in which hard work and deprivation were worshiped.

Camille's dad taught her that service and hard work were divine and money and status were evil. "How do you go against a code like that?" she asked with a deep sigh. "People who lived in nice homes and earned good salaries were considered uppity in our family. I remember my dad telling my brother over and over not to get too big for his britches.

"Johnny must have taken that in real deep. He's had assembly line jobs his whole life—over thirty years—even though he had a tremendous talent for inventing things. Our whole family was so full of shame, I was terrified to stand out in a crowd for fear of what my parents would think of me. I don't want to be noticed, and I've made sure of that by the way I dress and the jobs I pick. Most of my adult life I've worked in a kitchen, wearing a white uniform and a hair net!"

BAREFOOT AND BROKE

"There is a subtle belief in our culture," says Sondra Mehlhop, "that women are to be the heart of the home and men are to be the competitors—the ones out there slaying the dragons and bringing home the bacon. Intellectually women may believe they are coequals, as capable and motivated as men, but subconsciously I think many have bought into the 'barefoot and pregnant' syndrome."

Many of us believe somehow that it's better to go along with a society that says men have the status and power than to test our mettle by pushing against it. In addition, "there are few models for women in the area of financial success," said Mehlhop.

Even wealthy women like Joan Kroc, wife of the late Ray Kroc of the McDonald's fast food empire, and Jackie Kennedy Onassis are not true role models, since their wealth came through their husbands. Yet these women are respected and admired in our culture in a way that the high-powered, high-earning female is not.

MEANWHILE, BACK TO THE CLASSROOM . . .

Irene Freeman, president of Consumer Credit Counselors in San Diego, agrees.[1] "Boys get more financial education than girls in our society, partly because of the white-Anglo success stories of men like Forbes and Trump and Rockefeller. But girls don't hear about the female counterparts. Or if they do hear of one, she is often viewed as a person who criticizes and controls, and is generally male-oriented in her personality and behavior."

Freeman, who oversees a nonprofit credit counseling agency for consumers, says, "There is truly no integrated system of teaching personal economics to boys and girls while growing up. It's frightening to see how little money sense is taught in our schools." Then smiling wryly, she adds, "Sex education has finally come into the schools. Money has not!"

Mehlhop agrees. "Even in 1990 the salaries in the marketplace were still not equal for men and women. Men start their careers at a higher level and continue to earn more than women over their working lives. So there is some reality to a woman's fear of not being able to earn what she needs. But setting that aside for the moment, I believe that the love addiction and the codependence-dependence that occurs in relationships has a lot to do with this experience. It keeps many women from feeling adequate without a man. 'Money,' as the saying goes, 'does not warm you at night'—nor does one's career."

Women seem to have bought the notion that they can't have both. Yet, often men make such a choice—for the same reasons. This is not to say that every woman has to earn money in order to feel like a whole person, but these and other professionals are suggesting that women would benefit in every way from accepting more responsibility for their lives—including the financial aspects.

Choosing not to work for a time—while raising children, for example—could be just as responsible a financial decision as going into a high-paying career full-time. The measure of one's worth, then, is not the job we do or the dollars we earn, but the overall attitude and viewpoint we assume about our well-being. Making an informed decision often makes the difference between feeling empowered or powerless.

SELF-FULFILLING PROPHECY

Susan McKean, a certified financial planner in La Jolla, California,[2] and a Christian, says that "acquiring financial knowledge and then positively applying it to one's life is really a way of saying, 'I'm willing to be responsible for my own life.' Maybe no one is ever 100 percent responsible, since there's always at least one little place where we're vulnerable, but we can assume the majority of responsibility."

McKean, attractive and well-groomed, spoke frankly about her business of helping people with their financial affairs. She too sees a number of women who have never earned, or who do not earn what they need. "They have devoted themselves to raising their families, and they now believe they can't earn very much anyway, so why put forth the effort?"

Their decision to stay at home, then, was not a conscious choice as a part of their overall life plan, but rather something they did by default or as a result of a family pattern or because of someone else's expectations for them. Such women are not empowered by this experience; instead, they are often debilitated by it.

Freeman, a confident middle-aged woman with a generous smile, speaks easily about her experience with women in debt. She said that in her observation "many of us start our lives backwards. We never truly define the lifestyle we want. We let life happen to us. We make other people's dreams our dreams. But this doesn't have to be the case," she said with a note of hope. "We can become educated to a new way of thinking and behaving."

DEFINING SUCCESS

Education is one of the primary services of Consumer Credit Counselors. Freeman strongly believes that women need to be encouraged to "define success for themselves by establishing goals and then finding out how to go about achieving them."

Susan McKean agrees. "The process of learning is important," she said. "Personally, I enjoy it. We need to identify and learn how to state what we want, where we are going, how we wish to get there—and then be able to measure our progress."

McKean works with her clients in a practical way. "One of the tools I like to use is lists. I have a woman write down her goals on one list, then in another list, write down her emotional response to each one. For example, if her goal is to buy a new car in six months, she also writes down how she wants to feel about it. Perhaps her goal is to feel good about her ability to research and negotiate an auto loan by herself, or she may admit that she's scared of buying a new car because she realizes it means having to save a certain amount of money each month for that purpose." It might also be a catalyst to encourage a woman who has a low-paying job to consider alternative ways to earn additional income.

EMOTIONAL PROTECTION

I remember a time in my own life when my freelance income dropped below my need level for over a year, and I became depressed and frustrated. I didn't want to give up my own business to work for someone else, yet I felt powerless to turn my situation around.

I met with two friends in a recovery group I attend, and they helped me brainstorm about how I could raise my income. I listed my income goals, the ways in which I thought I could earn the additional money, and how and where I could make it happen. During the process, I suddenly realized that I could organize two support groups for writers in my home and charge a certain amount per month for regular attendance. Within three months I had my program launched. I've been doing this for over a year now and have added up to $1,000 each month to my income. As I reflect on this now, I'm struck by the fact that this $12,000 sum was beyond my reach until I was willing to look at the possibilities and receive the support and encouragement of trusted friends.

Many women who under-earn find that low-paying jobs actually provide a form of emotional protection they are afraid to give up. "As long as I'm living on the edge, I don't have the time or energy to look at what I'd really like to do with my life," said Brianna.

"I talk a lot about getting a better job," said Wilma, "but I haven't taken one step toward it. I'm not sure I'd know how to start. I don't know the first thing about putting a resume together or marketing myself. It's overwhelming." Meanwhile, Wilma is a file clerk in an office, earning $6.00 an hour.

A QUESTION OF ATTITUDE

These situations, coupled with cultural influences, set up many women, who already suffer from lack of confidence or low self-esteem, to remain jobless or to take work that will keep them financially suppressed.

Because of the socialization process Mehlhop spoke of, many women deliberately under-earn, clinging to the belief that it is the male's role to provide for them financially—even after a divorce. Others, like Dianne and Suzanne and Laurel in previous chapters, were raised to believe that it was unthinkable for women to work. Therefore, even the thought of looking for or qualifying for a satisfying job that pays adequately can be overwhelming.

McKean said that some of the female divorce victims she works with "want to make life difficult for their ex-husbands or heap guilt on them." They may use under-earning or not working as a way to make the men suffer. "But I see how this attitude hurts a woman," said McKean. "She isn't getting on with her life. Actually it's handicapping *her,* because he usually goes on with his plans no matter what happens."

McKean said that when she started her business she wanted to save all her clients. "I thought that if I just showed up and had a plan, we'd all live happily ever after. Since then I've stepped back, and I now believe very strongly in educating my clients, guiding them, providing structure and whatever else they need, but I will not take responsibility for them."

Now that McKean has a more realistic view of how to counsel her clients, she is free to enjoy the result. "One of the most satisfying things about my work," she said, "is seeing people grow and become more aware of the possibilities."

McKean also strongly believes that for her, spiritual growth was an important aspect of working through financial problems. "It's a very big part of my life," she said, "something that I hope comes through in the way I work with people." McKean knows from her own life how frightening it can be to face one's financial obligations alone following a divorce.

"I wouldn't be the person I am today without God," she said. "I think sometimes I frustrate Him to the nth degree, however, because I have put a lot of stumbling blocks in my own way. But He has taught me when I see a boulder in the road, not to view it as an obstruction, but instead, to climb up on top of it in order to see down the road. And He has *always* been on the other side of that boulder, a very comforting thing to know."

McKean believes it's very difficult to be a woman today, to be divorced or widowed or single, to develop job skills, to be a mother and a wage earner and not develop a negative attitude. "A positive attitude is something you have to work at consciously, day by day, whether you're successful or not. We all have down times when things don't go our way. It all comes down to how we elect to approach them and the attitude we choose."

BY CHOICE, NOT BY CHANCE

A woman who is willing to grow is also usually willing to establish a plan for her life. She looks at long-range and short-term goals. She may choose to remain at home for ten to twenty years to rear her children and she commits to that plan—but she doesn't let it ground her for life. She views it for what it is—a *portion* of her life—and she may even use some of that time to prepare herself for the years after her children are grown. Such a woman is demonstrating responsibility for her life, even though she may not be a full-time wage earner.

Others choose to work two or three days a week in a profession that does not demand a full-week commitment, allowing the remaining time for family affairs. When my children were in the primary grades, I worked about ten hours a week in my home as a language arts and math tutor.

Another woman did something similar with her talent. She taught needlepoint in her home two mornings a week. Years later, when her children were more independent, she opened her own needlework shop.

A friend of mine started a travel agency after her two boys entered high school. Prior to that she remained at home, but she prepared for the future by studying the travel business and getting her license.

Under-earning is not a condition that must be endured or a position in life that a woman has no control over. Feeling good about our ability to earn and manage a salary is as important to our total health as are the physical, spiritual, mental, and emotional aspects.

Those of us overwhelmed by fear and low self-esteem can become willing, through prayer and counseling and group therapy, to embrace the belief that we are worthy of an income that rewards and supports us appropriately.

I hope the following stories of four women who have struggled with under-earning and who are now in recovery will encourage you as you discover and reach out for what you really want, need, and deserve.

No More Crumbs: Caren's Story

Caren grew up "taking the crumbs." She remembers as a teenager helping out her mother with her own earnings, because she never saw her mother pay the bills. "I picked up the slack and took care of my sisters. The problem was, there was nothing left for me. I never learned to take care of myself because no one taught me how."

Today Caren struggles with overeating and low self-esteem. As we talked I noticed what a lovely, open face she has and how generous she is. But Caren is just beginning to see the good in herself.

Her mother instilled in her the belief that "if you have something good, you should give it away." This belief colored most of Caren's actions throughout her youth. And as an adult she perpetuated this childhood pattern.

"Whenever I applied for a job, I'd set up interviews for the lower-paying work. I have always played down my talents, what I wanted, or what I was earning at a former job." Caren had no education when it came to earning or managing money. "I married at eighteen, and my husband took over the finances. And I had to do whatever he wanted in order to get any money."

Caren admitted that she has been in denial for so long it's frightening. "Until recently I've had no sense of personal responsibility. My parents died young—ages sixty-two and sixty-four—and I've worried that I might die early, like them. So my attitude has been that it's better to live now and have things now." As a result, she's had a real struggle holding on to any money at all. "The only way I can save is through a payroll deduction," she said, "and even that doesn't guarantee that it will stay there."

After Caren's parents died she inherited $25,000, which she spent on a variety of things, including a trip to Europe. Once again, she felt the need to spend it, to get rid of it, to keep it away because she was too scared to deal with it.

Caren's ex-husband confirmed her suspicions by telling her when they separated that she'd "never make it for more than two weeks by herself." Interestingly, she has made it for seven years, though it has not been easy. On the other hand, she claims she has also continued to prove her ex-husband right by missing credit payments, under-earning, and living on the edge—"shameful acts," she calls them.

Caren has also continued her early pattern of giving to everyone but herself, including her creditors. "When I pay a large bill, like Visa, I get a rush from paying it off. I get myself into the mess, and then I feel triumphant when I get myself out. But again, there's nothing left for me. I've had so much resistance to receiving good, I even lost the notebook for a prosperity course I signed up for."

However, she's beginning to see some changes. "At one time I couldn't even treat myself to a movie. Now I can do something nice for myself once in a while and not feel guilty about it."

Caren has made tremendous progress in her career path over the last year. For months she had a telephone partner whom she called every day for prayer and support. After months without any work at all, creditors hounding her, and the threat of foreclosure on her two-bedroom condominium, she took a job in telemarketing for little over minimum wage.

Then miraculously one of the import-export businesses she had previously contacted hired her as a traffic coordinator in the international shipping department. She has a regular paycheck again, opportunity for advancement, and a sense of well-being about her ability and her worth as an employee.

Caren receives all this good with some caution, however. "I still sabotage myself in many ways. I spend money on my daughter when she visits, even when I don't have it, and I find myself wanting to donate to charities when I barely have the house payment for that month. I find all sorts of reasons for charging one more thing on my Visa card when I'm already thousands of dollars in debt.

"I play little games with myself, taking from one account to pay another. And when it gets overwhelming, I eat or shop or go on a little trip. I know I'm still confused about my reality. I don't have a good sense of balance yet."

Then, on a more hopeful note and with a warm smile, she added, "But I'm now reaching out for people in Debtors Anonymous. And it's working. I'm beginning to see the power of human compassion to ward off compulsions."

The Root of All Evil: Chris's Story

One of Chris's earliest memories associated with money goes back to her eighth year. "I had a job weeding dandelions from people's yards," she said, "and I was paid by the pailful. I remember cheating by filling the pail with mowed grass and then putting the dandelions on top."

Chris also recalls a time when she stole all the Christmas presents she wanted to give to her family from the five-and-dime store. "I'm not sure why," she said.

Then, reflecting for a moment, she added, "The belief in our home was that money is the root of all evil. None of us—myself, three sisters, and one brother—grew up wanting to make money.

"We watched our dad spend most of his life under-earning. He never did what he really wanted to do, despite the fact that he graduated from Harvard with honors. He worked for a newspaper, but what he really wanted was to be a published writer."

The family's way of dealing with money made a big impact on Chris's life. "I grew up believing that the only way to get more than the minimum was by chance. There were no savings. We never planned for emergencies or extras. My dad entered contests and sometimes won, but that was the only extra money we had. I also remember that my parents inherited my grandmother's furniture when she died."

Chris financed her own college education. "I paid part of the tuition with money I saved and the rest with student loans and part-time work as a student." She also received a partial scholarship.

"For the last twelve years, I've been an under-earner," said Chris, a warm and friendly woman, now in her late forties. Today only one of her five siblings is not in the same predicament.

In both her first and second marriages, the men were willing to go into debt. She went along with them, because "I didn't know there was any other way to have what I wanted and needed."

She perceived credit cards as her only option. "I charged everything from vacations to family trips, from medical bills to car care."

Chris continued this way until the amount of debt in her second marriage became overwhelming. That is what finally led her into a program for financial recovery. Prior to that time she had actually "begun thinking about getting more credit in order to have a better lifestyle. It never occurred to me," she said like a child discovering a secret, "that one could actually live one's life without debt. That was a totally novel idea to me when I first heard it."

She decided to give it a try. At the moment Chris and her husband have about $20,000 of debt, in addition to mortgages on two homes. They are in the process of working out a settlement prior to their divorce.

"I feel a lot of pain when I see how much I have deprived myself by being an under-earner. But I also have a hunch," she added with a smile, "that within the next couple of years I'll be out of that pattern." Chris now works as a word processor, but her training and real love is in the field of social work. She hopes to return to that work within the next year.

"I now know how to live within my means more than ever before. I keep meeting people who support me in remaining debt-free. I've traded personal items for car repairs. I do volunteer work a couple of hours a month in a food-share program in exchange for groceries at a special discount, and I even gave a party and stayed within my spending plan by using paper goods I had on hand and inviting each guest to bring food to share."

Chris is grateful to the principles of the Debtors Anonymous program for helping her discover how to live within her means because it has stimulated her creativity. "I'm now willing to play my violin for pleasure, listen to books on tape as I drive, and take care of my plants"—activities she rarely indulged in before because of her preoccupation with living on the edge.

"I used to believe it was wrong for me to earn more than I needed to subsist, especially when so many people don't even have jobs. But since then I've come to realize that others can't be helped by my earning less. Only *my* circumstances are affected. And I also see that most people are where they are because of what they believe or think. I can be more inspiring to others by taking care of myself first."

Chris was an atheist before she entered her first recovery program—for overeating. Today she has a personal relationship with God. "I see that God has good for me," she said, her eyes glowing softly, "and so I am more conscious of asking for His guidance."

All or Nothing: Miki's Story

Miki, a petite thirty-year-old with long, sand-colored hair, is also an under-earner by her own definition. "The binge-splurge cycle and the all-or-nothing mentality have run my life," she said. "I'm forever putting out fires, spending what I don't have, breaking my commitments. Then out of resentment I spend more, telling myself I deserve something."

Miki has been an under-earner during all of her working life. "I believe it revolves around resentment. I left home at age eighteen in rebellion against my parents. I didn't have the skills then to live on my own. And I've just never caught up." Miki's mother cautioned her to pay her bills and establish good credit but didn't show her how to do either one.

Her dad never pursued his dreams, and as a result, Miki believes "he used his kids as scapegoats. Both my parents blamed us for their problems."

After Miki left home she looked into living in a commune because she "didn't want to be a part of society. I had no knowledge of how to live in the world."

Today she has a part-time bookkeeping and freelance writing business. "I learned to keep books by working with a friend of the family. Basically, I had an affinity for the work, and the rest I faked," she said with an embarrassed laugh.

She also had a job in an auto parts store and worked as a waitress. "Most of the time I lied to get jobs. I'd give references of places that had closed down."

Miki also admitted to stealing up to $2,000 over an extended period in order to make ends meet. "I had access to petty cash, and I always stole with the intention of paying it back. But then I'd need the money to meet basic expenses, critical things like utilities that were on the verge of being shut off."

At one time she received $3,000 as a gift from her grandmother. "I wanted to use it to buy a house, but I didn't have enough for the down payment, so I frittered it away, writing checks for whatever I wanted until there was nothing left."

Miki was also terrified to ask her husband for money, because she was so ashamed of what she had done and because they had never talked about money.

Miki believes that some of her insanity with money has come down the generations. Her dad's father was a wealthy man who was considered a "bootstraps type of guy. He made a lot of money, then lost it. He was also diagnosed as manic depressive and drove himself crazy over not being able to pay his bills."

Miki remembers believing while growing up that money was no good. "It killed my grandfather." At the same time she's had some deep conflicts. "I have a strong drive to have nice things. It takes money to buy them. But since, to me, money was no good, I kept myself earning less than I needed and then felt deprived. I'd spend to feel better, get into debt, and the cycle would start all over again."

Today, in recovery, Miki reminds herself that she has been sick around money for a long time. "I need to remember that it's going to take more time to get well. I keep telling myself I am *convalescing.*

"Today I'm willing to do it God's way. I did it my way for fifteen years, and it didn't work. A person can white-knuckle it for just so long."

Never Enough: Tammy's Story

Tammy, a bright, animated woman of thirty-five, who is an artist and an art consultant, is doing the work she loves—but she's also an under-earner. She comes from a family who lived in survival during her entire childhood.

"My dad had his own business," she said, "and always had financial problems. He managed to pay his employees, but there was barely enough for him. There were seven kids in the family, and we pinched pennies for as long as I can remember."

Tammy remembers coming home with a list of supplies needed for school, and she couldn't even have a new box of crayons, because there wasn't enough money.

"There was never any spending money for us kids, so we all worked. Four of the kids had paper routes. I got a job through my sister at Dairy Queen when I was fifteen, and I continued working from that point on. During college I worked as a waitress and as a clerk in a retail store. I worked twice as hard as a lot of people I knew, because I always took low-paying jobs."

Tammy believes her dad's fear of success sabotaged him and the entire family. "He never knew how to handle money," she said.

Today Tammy sees how these patterns and beliefs have affected her work as an artist. She does commissioned pieces of art for businesses and individuals. She has done a super-graphic in a men's gym, contemporary abstract pieces for businesses and individuals, and custom jewelry. "I don't ask enough for these jobs. Too often I've worked without being paid." It's customary in Tammy's field to request a deposit before starting a job, but she admits that she is "afraid to ask for 50 percent up front."

As a result of not earning enough, Tammy is still struggling with credit cards. "I have only two left," she said, "and I'm making monthly payments without adding any new debt." At this time Tammy attends recovery group meetings and is learning to take life less seriously. "I can deal with it now. And my self-esteem is higher. Under-earning is such a classic thing for a woman. I would advise any woman to take care of herself and to learn about money, so she can earn what she deserves and feel good about herself."

Taking Inventory

Women who under-earn answer "often" or "very often" to many of these statements:

1. I don't feel I deserve more than minimum wage.

2. I'm afraid I won't be able to make work-related decisions that affect other people.

3. I'm afraid of failure.

4. I'm afraid of what success would entail.

5. I'm not trained or educated enough for the work world.

6. I'm too old to start over.

7. I'm afraid of competition.

8. I'm afraid to make a commitment to a job.

9. I don't want to be noticed.

10. I feel inadequate when applying for a job.

11. I don't know what I really want to do.

12. I want someone else to take care of me.

9

Self-debtors

Many women in debt continually reject or manipulate their environments in order to avoid experiencing the pain of loss and neglect they felt as children. They are chronic self-debtors—women who are in debt to themselves physically, spiritually, mentally, emotionally, and financially. Although they have many traits in common with other women in debt, they differ in three distinct ways.

Self-debtors cannot give to themselves without feeling enormous guilt.

In extreme cases, they cannot give to themselves at all. Self-debtors of this magnitude often end up on the street like Pearl did. She is an intelligent, educated woman, who at one time was homeless.

As we talked, she sobbed. Then she slammed her fist on the table. "When am I going to stop this?" Pearl shouted. "I feel so guilty if I do one small thing for myself. I can't say no to my friends, to my neighbors, to the people I work with—and most of all to my mother."

Here was a fifty-nine-year-old woman still being run by her mother—a frail, white-haired lady of eighty-two. Yet she wielded more power than the board of directors of a Fortune 500 company. She called Pearl every day at work at least three or four times. Her list of needs and emergencies was endless. And her demand for time and service while Pearl was home appeared to be insatiable.

Pearl's mother had always used her poor health as a weapon. "She's been 'dying' for fifty years," Pearl said, between laughing and crying. "Now I'm taking care of her physically and financially. And she never says thank you. She seems to feel it's my duty as her daughter."

The only break Pearl gets is when she does volunteer work at the art museum or baby-sits during a Sunday service at her church. She thinks, "The only thing I'm good at is taking care of people."

Pearl is also in financial debt. She spends her money on others—gifts for friends, the children in Sunday school, her mother—while neglecting her own most basic needs. Recently she began attending meetings of Debtors Anonymous, after a co-worker suggested the group as a means of support.

"I even had to think twice about going to DA. I felt as though I ought to be able to handle my own problems. But I just can't anymore," she said as she lowered her head and sobbed again. "I'm out of control."

It was no surprise to find out that Pearl works as a nurses' aide in a hospital. Even her job is an expression of the caretaking role she learned while growing up.

Pearl is a classic self-debtor. Her sense of worth and well-being comes from helping others. Meanwhile Pearl's physical and emotional health go unattended and her debts mount as she spends her money and energy on everyone but herself.

They reject attention even though they crave it.

Self-debtors usually arrange their lives in a way that keeps love and warmth at a distance so they will not be reminded of the deprivation they experienced as children. They manage or manipulate others in order to keep from having to look at themselves and their need for real intimacy.

At the same time they crave attention and are obsessed with the fact that people do not notice them, take them for granted, don't acknowledge them, and never say thank you.

"Self-debt is not as apparent a behavior as compulsive shopping or gambling," said Rusty, a forty-seven-year-old secretary. "You can put your mind around something that specific and go for help."

She shifted in her chair, then spoke again. "I never knew that I was keeping people away by doing things for them. I took pride in putting others first. That's the way I was brought up. Whenever I expressed myself, like saying how I was feeling or asking for something I wanted, my mother and my grandmother would jump all over me. They instilled in me the idea of putting other people ahead of myself. Pretty soon I believed that was right.

I noticed a painful expression in Rusty's eyes as she continued. "When I was in grade school I wanted to be the person who led the flag salute," she said, "or be the announcer on parent night. But I honestly believed someone else could do it better."

As Rusty got older she avoided competition and confrontation. She was actually afraid to win a game or a trophy or be in the spotlight for any reason. And she was scared of expressing her opinion or her feelings. "At the same time, I was dying to be chosen. I used to dream about getting the best part in a school play or being voted class president."

Rusty admitted that she's the same way today. She's more comfortable behind the scenes than on stage. She'd rather sew costumes for others than wear one herself. She prefers to type a report rather than give one. But she also fantasizes about the day she'll get a community service award or be voted the employee of the month at work.

Rusty wants recognition, but she carefully avoids putting herself in a place where she will be noticed. She has convinced people that she is happy just the way she is. And they don't argue with her. But Rusty is angry with them. She wants them to pay attention to *her* for a change.

They steal from themselves to give to others.

Jolene, a thirty-eight-year-old single entrepreneur, has a serious problem but feels powerless over it. "I feel guilty turning down a good cause or a committee that's going to help children, or save pets, or keep a young mother from aborting her baby. I've been blessed, so I feel like the least I can do is give my time and money. I can always make up for it later, when I'm older."

Jolene looked away for a moment, then returned to the conversation. "But I've been saying that for twenty years," she said with a touch of self-directed sarcasm.

Jolene didn't wake up to her problem of self-debt until she began to feel it financially. Her catering business dipped dramatically because she took so much time off. "I also lost a lot of jobs because I wasn't home to take calls, or I didn't return them soon enough to get the orders."

For a time Jolene was volunteering ten to fifteen hours a week and squeezing her business into what was left. Not only was she losing necessary income, but her personal life began to suffer as well. "I didn't go to the dentist. I didn't eat properly. I didn't water my plants or clean my apartment or take a walk. Everything I did involved other people."

Many women in debt gradually learn that even though they are in financial debt to others, their biggest creditor is themselves. "I'm just beginning to see that I owe myself far more than I owe anyone else," said Jolene. "I have not been a good friend to myself."

Marilyn, Jeannie, and Marcie might say the same thing about themselves. Marilyn abandoned herself through overspending and a self-indulgent lifestyle, and now she's in debt. Jeannie's self-debting issues have revolved around her relationships with men and money. And Marcie has expressed her self-debt through caretaking and under-earning. Their stories are next.

The Princess Syndrome: Marilyn's Story

When it comes to money, Marilyn, an attractive and energetic school teacher in her mid-forties, says she has no money. "I'm like the alcoholic who downs ten drinks but swears she had only two. I'll spend $200, and yet firmly believe I've spent only $50. I have no reality, no awareness of the numbers. I've gone for two months or more without balancing my checkbook."

Marilyn's former husband bailed her out of debt again and again, yet he used money to blackmail her. She often felt helpless in the marriage because their lifestyle was the result of his earning. "I had no money of my own, but at the same time I didn't have to *do* anything. I lived like a princess. We had a live-in maid, a second house in Lake Arrowhead, California, nice cars, membership in a country club."

Marilyn also remained in denial by avoiding any information about their financial affairs. "I didn't want to know anything about money during those years. I signed the tax returns without even looking at them. Money kept me in that marriage.

"I thought it was a good life—parties, friends, a nice lifestyle. On one hand I was taken care of, but I hurt myself by staying in a marriage with a manic-depressive, mentally ill man who used his wealth to manipulate me. And I stayed because I didn't want to give up our lifestyle." Marilyn didn't believe she could create that kind of a life on her own.

"I don't know where all this comes from," she said openly. "I'm in therapy now to deal with the root causes of these issues. My father came from a shame-based family. He took over for his dad at a young age."

While Marilyn was growing up, her father provided her with nice things. "Appearances were very important in our family, and love was extremely conditional. I always looked to outside sources for confirmation that I was all right. To this day, how I look is very important to me."

Marilyn's life now seems pretty bleak when compared with earlier years. Her husband lost his business, and divorce followed. She married again, but the marriage lasted only fourteen months and left her in financial ruin. "I took out a second mortgage on my house to pay off his debts—$48,000 worth of unsecured debt. I think I felt that if I took care of him financially he'd stay. When I don't feel I'm enough of a person, I try to hold on. But it didn't work."

After a divorce that cost her $7,000 on top of the huge loan, Marilyn hit bottom. "The truth was finally out. No one cared for me. No one ever had. There would be no one to meet my emotional needs."

During the same period, Marilyn's son entered drug rehabilitation and her teen-aged daughter was assaulted and raped. She put her house on the market, opening and closing escrows on her own.

"Suddenly I went into overload," she said, her voice escalating with emotion. "I thought I would die. I felt totally trapped. I couldn't see any options. I stopped all my responsibilities. For a long time I just lived day to day. Then, for a time, I got involved in Overeaters Anonymous. But what I was really searching for was a Twelve Step program that deals with debt."

Marilyn paused, took a deep breath, and continued. "I was persistent about that and finally I found it. Now after more than a year in Debtors Anonymous, I can say that I see I am capable of doing something good for myself. I am trying to deal with my pain. Rather than covering it as I did for so many years, I am facing it and looking beneath it. I see now that all my obsessing about money, my checkbook, and my debts was one of my ways of coping. It took the place of feeling the pain."

Today Marilyn's image of herself is being healed. "God has shown me that He will provide, but I'm still scared to trust. I have a horrible fear that He won't come through the next time. Even though that fear is not based on reality or experience.

"Years ago when I was in my early twenties and coming out of a very bad situation, God gave me a Bible verse that I have clung to: 'My God shall supply all your needs.' "

Marilyn recalls how God made good on that promise when she trusted Him for His provision for tuition and board at Western Michigan University. She had applied for an on-campus job as assistant dormitory director but was told that kind of position was not available to first-year students.

Yet, that very day a letter arrived confirming a full-tuition scholarship. God had taken her that far. She knew He wouldn't desert her then. Within days of that letter, the Lord delivered another miracle. The position of assistant dorm director opened up unexpectedly, and she was called for an interview. "I got the job," she said excitedly, "and it included even more than I had hoped for—a private suite, meals, free housekeeping, a parking place, my own key to the place, and I had every other weekend off."

Today Marilyn's debt is down to $15,000. She owes $12,000 to credit card companies, $2,000 to her mother, and $1,000 to her aunt. The Lord appears to be fulfilling his promise to Marilyn once again.

No-Talk Family: Jeannie's Story

"I was the last of my parents' three daughters," said Jeannie, a slim, soft-spoken woman in her early forties. "My mother was thirty-eight and my dad forty-six when I was born. I was part of the best years of their lives. When we moved across country from Illinois to California, they built a house for the first time. I remember the love and excitement there. We even had a birthday party for the house.

"I never noticed any financial struggle during that time. My sisters and I could decorate our rooms the way we wanted. I even went to the nursery with my parents and picked out my own chrysanthemum for the yard."

Jeannie's father was the major earner. "He was an electrical engineer and happy in his work at Lockheed Aircraft Corporation. I remember thinking we had the nicest house in the neighborhood, the nicest cars, and my dad had the nicest job. I learned about money from him.

"My mother was a pleasant woman, strong and energetic. When I was ten I thought my mom had a great deal. She could go to the pool with me because she didn't have to work like some of the other women in the neighborhood."

Jeannie's idyllic life continued into junior high, where she was very popular, was involved in various service organizations, and rode horses in the country. "It was the perfect background, until high school. Then everything changed. I had to go to a school where the kids were upper middle class and more mature than I was. I was not like them."

It was then that Jeannie began to see another side of life—a side she wasn't used to and one she didn't feel comfortable with. "My mother had always made my clothes," said Jeannie. "In fact, it wasn't until tenth grade that I bought my first piece of clothing in a store. It was a marshmallow crepe blouse."

The new blouse gave Jeannie such a sense of prosperity she decided then to build a wardrobe. For a period of time after that, however, she went "back and forth between plenty and lack." These early signs of self-debting may have influenced her patterns with money and self-care later in her life.

Her most turbulent years were between seventeen and twenty-four. "I was involved with a boy who was really wealthy, but I didn't see how our relationship could last un-

less I had money too. So we broke up, and I was devastated."
In looking back, Jeannie sees how much power she attached
to money.

Her next move was across the world. She went to Australia
for several years and became a successful teacher. That career came to an end, however, when she received word that
her mother was seriously ill. Jeannie flew home to see her and
stayed on with her father after her mother died. "It was a very
stressful time. He was trying to deal with his loss, and I was
trying to help him. Neither one of us had any tools. We had
always been a 'no-talk' family, and we still were."

During that time Jeannie met Will, the man she later married. "We lived together for a while, and then for a time I
moved back home with Dad. It was a terrible time for me. Both
Dad and Will seemed to be fighting over me. And I was so
needy I didn't know how to take care of myself."

One of the first things Jeannie did was to become financially
enmeshed with Will. "I felt a lot of shame around money issues, because I had never had much money of my own. I
didn't know how to earn enough to meet my needs, and I
didn't know how to manage what I did have."

Will had similar problems. "When we met we were both in
debt, and struggling." As Jeannie reflected on those years
now, she said on a wistful note, "I wanted him to take care of
me financially, and now I realize he may have wanted me to
take care of him."

Her biggest fear was that she wouldn't be protected. "We
bought a house and started a business together. We used my
money to create this enterprise; yet I couldn't believe I could
have it without him. It was crazy.

"I became a cloying, desperate woman. As soon as any feelings of abandonment came up, I wanted to get married. I
learned when I met him that he had been struggling with a
major addiction, yet I married him anyway. I was so sure I
couldn't handle life on my own."

For a while Jeannie and Will lived in Japan, so Will could
study art. "Again, I financed the whole thing," she said. "Then
when I wanted to go to India to study yoga, I dropped my
plans because I didn't believe we had enough money for *me* to
do *my* thing."

Jeannie and Will's relationship followed that pattern for

years. When it came to her needs, there was never enough, not because Will denied her, but because she denied herself.

The fellowship of Debtors Anonymous means a lot to Jeannie today. Through its program she has discovered that what appeared to be money issues actually goes much deeper. They have to do with her worth and well-being as a woman. "Recovery is—well, slow-going," said Jeannie with hesitation in her voice. "I have a lot of shame—even more shame as my denial lifts."

She is having success, however, practicing the principles of DA and using the tools of recovery, which include keeping track of her expenses, cutting up her credit cards, attending meetings, and putting a spending plan together. "Actually my problems with money reflect deeper issues that I'm just beginning to look at seriously. Money was a place to start. It helped me get going."

Today Jeannie is sharing her pain with other women in debt. She is talking about it now, and expressing her deepest feelings—a healthy sign for someone who came from a "no-talk" family.

Good Little Mommy: Marcie's Story

"I was the second oldest child of seven and the oldest girl." Marcie's no-nonsense manner is a disarming contrast to her inviting smile and fabulous curly hair. Behind the pretty looks, however, is a woman who knows pain, someone who grew up fast and assumed adult responsibilities long before her time.

"My mother was an alcoholic, and my dad a workaholic. He always had two or three jobs going at once. They were divorced when I was twelve."

That year Marcie's childhood in Columbus, Ohio, came to an end. "We didn't see much of our dad after that. He rarely called, and he didn't visit us except on our birthdays, when he'd take the birthday person out for dinner.

"Since my dad had had an affair, my mother set out to prove her sexual appeal after they were divorced. She was young—only thirty-three—and she had seven kids. She decided she wanted to have a life. She worked, bowled, partied, and rarely slept at home. I became the surrogate mom, and my younger brother became the surrogate dad. And later he became a heroin addict."

Marcie believes her problems with money started around that time. "My mother would give me $5 a day to feed seven kids. That was my first experience with juggling money—and I still do it to this day." Marcie panhandled as a kid to bring in a few extra dollars. "At the time I didn't even know I was begging."

Marcie has other remembrances of money from her childhood. When she was six or seven, a cousin taught her to take money from her mother's purse. "There was never enough for everyone in the family. The tennis shoes I wanted were too expensive, so I had to do without or settle for a very cheap pair—something I thought normal kids didn't have to do. It made me feel I was less than normal."

When Marcie began dating she was slow to let go of the reins on money. "I tried to pay for movies and food, even if I didn't have to." Later, when she married and left home, she continued her role as caretaker, and the self-debt increased. "I was the top student in trade school. I got a full-time job because I knew I'd need it—even though at the time I married it was the norm for the husband to work full-time and the wife part-time.

"My mother's message to me was 'Don't ever expect money from men.' " So Marcie didn't. "I took control. I didn't want the men in my life to work, or they might leave me." Her first husband obliged, whether he realized it or not. He had fifteen jobs in twelve years.

Marcie's dad also used money to control his children as adults. For example, "One year he wanted to buy me furniture as a house-warming present. He bought a couch, love seat, two chairs, and a coffee table at an estate sale. He was trying to please me," she said, smiling, "but he obviously didn't know me. His choices were dark, depressing antiques. I wanted floral prints," she said, her tone lightening as she spoke, "to reflect my recovering self."

Her dad was relating to Marcie's old self. "He only knew what he had created—someone who would please him and be forever grateful. His message was 'Don't be who you are, be who I want you to be.' He always called me 'a good little mommy.'

10

Perpetual Paupers

At the opposite end of the debt spectrum are perpetual paupers—women who are compelled to push whatever money they have. These individuals *must* get of their money as fast as it comes in. They are not necessarily overspenders, although they might be, and they do not necessarily use credit cards. They might not owe anyone anything. Spending money on themselves may not be a problem them as it is for self-debtors. They might not gamble, shop, and in excess, or under-earn, but nonetheless they are women in debt.

Paupers cannot keep money. They cannot save it, invest it, hold on to it in any form. They are compelled to live on the edge.

The women I spoke with who identify with this behavior and this disorder is as baffling to them as it is to those around them who observe it. Many make enough money to meet their needs and wants, but get rid of it as fast as they earn it with thought of what is really important to them. Some are under-earners, also an expression of their compulsion to keep money at a distance. And still others are flat broke all the time, working intermittently, squandering or giving away what does come in, and generally living a hand-to-mouth existence, even though a better life is possible. Several traits seem to characterize the perpetual pauper.

"My dad was a 'coupon person.' He never bought anything unless it was a good deal. I remember him driving 100 miles once to bring me a coupon."

Marcie sees herself repeating the family pattern today. She was divorced after eleven years of marriage at the same age as her mother when she and Marcie's dad were divorced. The one difference, however, is that she and her two children are in recovery.

Still, breaking old patterns does not come easy. "I hurt myself by bingeing and purging with money. I'm trying to identify what I do, and, for example, why I let my bills go for two months at a time."

Marcie is also trying for the first time to learn about nutrition. "I was never taught how to cook or eat properly. I know we eat out too much, but I get sick of cooking. Maybe I'm making up for the past when I had to do all the cooking."

Housekeeping, cooking, and bill-paying also stir up painful memories. "When money is tight, it brings up thoughts that there won't be enough. I remember as a kid that by the time I got to the table after cooking for my brothers and sisters there was no food left for me."

Marcie also sabotaged herself by using food to help her deal with grief. When she learned that her brother had committed suicide, she handled the overwhelming feelings by eating out or heating up a TV dinner. "I've operated on the belief that I had better eat what I can or there won't be enough for me."

She was also the "family hero." Once she gave $1,000 to a woman who needed it—even though Marcie needed it just as much or more. She is also an incest survivor and a workaholic. "I qualify for every Twelve Step program that was ever created," she said in a burst of laughter.

"I never planned anything in my whole life. Life always just happened to me. I have to trick myself in order to plan. I need to make myself face my 'busy' addiction, which I use to avoid doing what I *really* want to do. I want to play the piano," she said wistfully, "but I sold my piano for $50, because I needed the money." Marcie, like so many other self-debtors, has a hard time giving herself the things that really matter, because she keeps busy deflecting the pain of the past and its healing truth.

But Marcie is not willing to stay in pain and denial. She's in therapy now and attends several Twelve Step support groups. And she says she wants to build a relationship with God. "But the idea of a power greater than me is a difficult one, because for so long I was 'it'—the only one I could count on."

Today Marcie is taking what she calls baby steps. "I need to change jobs, but I feel stuck, paralyzed." Then she quickly changes her attitude and acknowledges herself for trying. "I bought a Sunday paper so I could read the want ads. I haven't opened it yet, but at least I bought it. That's a start."

FACING THE PAIN

To break the chain of self-debting behavior we have to move toward the truth about the past, the truth about our parents. Eventually we have to accept what we discover without blaming them. But this is a process that requires time, patience, and prayer, and often professional counseling as well.

Our parents did not give us the emotional nurturing we needed, because they didn't know how to or, more likely, because they did not receive from their parents the nurturing they needed. Only when we face this truth about our lives are we free to change our feelings, to alter our behavior, and to reject false beliefs from the past.

"God has given us pain as a sign that something is wrong and needs correction," says Rich Buhler in his marvelous book on victimization, *Pain and Pretending*.[1] "If I want to solve my problem," he says, "I frequently have to walk in the direction of the pain, not because I like pain but because I want to know the truth, which happens to be somewhere in the direction of the pain."

God did not intend for us to walk this path alone, however. Professional and spiritual help are available to anyone who reaches for them. There are licensed therapists who specialize in victimization and depression—common symptoms of self-debting. You can find names and phone numbers for these professionals through a church, a community mental health service, or a referral from someone you trust.

Taking Inventory

Women who are self-debtors answer "often" to these statements:

1. I always think of others before I think of my

2. I can't say no.

3. I crave attention, though I hide from it.

4. I focus on others, so I won't have to look at

5. I am quick to discount my own needs in orde ceptance.

6. I cannot give to myself without feeling guilty.

7. I have trouble making decisions that involve m

8. I spend money on others at the expense of my

An obsession with acquiring money

Amy, a thirty-one-year-old elementary school teacher, has a perfectly adequate salary and benefits, yet she has an exaggerated fear of economic insecurity. "I'm always looking for ways to get more money," she said. "I tutor reading students a couple of evenings a week. I teach English to a foreign student. I find myself planning ahead for money I know I'll receive for my birthday or Christmas. But no matter how much I have, it's never enough."

Simone can relate to this same compulsion. She donates blood to earn extra money when she's in need, and she and a friend take things to sell at a swap meet in their city. "I heard a lot of contradictory messages at home," said the smiling, soft-spoken thirty-year-old dressed in tattered blue jeans and T-shirt. "My mom handled the money in our family, and the message was 'We don't have enough.' But then every year before school started, it was better than Christmas. We got everything we needed and wanted." Simone believes "money covered the guilt my parents felt at not having a personal relationship with their kids. It was their currency of love."

An obsession with getting rid of it

At the same time that Amy and Simone are looking for ways to get more money, they also admit to their need to get rid of it by spending it or giving it away as fast as it comes in. "I'm a sucker for every charity that approaches me by phone or mail," said Amy. "I can't go to the grocery store without stocking up for months. There's a part of me that hoards stuff. I have enough toilet paper for a year, canned goods for months ahead of time, things like that—when the money could have been used to pay bills or to save for something really nice for myself. I'm always on the edge with money, struggling the last few days each month till payday. Sometimes I donate blood so I'll have gas money for my car."

Amy looks at other teachers she knows, and they seem to be fine. They have nice clothes and decent cars, and they take good vacations during their time off. "I *want* this for myself," she said, "but I have a hard time making it happen. One year I actually saved $200 in a special vacation account, but I felt restless every time the bank statement arrived. I felt like I should use it for something important."

She got her chance in December of that year when the brakes on her car went out and she had to spend her vacation fund on repairs. "I actually felt relieved to be drawing out that money. It had always seemed wrong somehow to have it just sitting there."

Simone remembers her first experience of "blowing all the money I had." She had saved $100 and "felt nervous and excited about spending it. I blew it all. And my mother was so disappointed in me, because she wanted me to save it for a rainy day."

As an adult, the cycle continued for Simone. "Until I got into recovery, I had almost no awareness of how to handle money, and I had a hard time seeing that I had choices."

Simone has a pauper compulsion. "I have to get rid of my money to make room for more. I feel that if I spend it, then I can have more." But as soon as more comes in, she spends that too, and the pattern repeats itself. And her mother has fed her disease. "She'd send money. I'd spend it. She'd get upset and then send me more. One time it would be $700; another time it would be $8,000."

Today Simone does not ask her parents for money for any reason. "I want to break the cycle," she said. "I want to be responsible for myself."

An obsession with abandoning the true self

Amy has abandoned her hopes and dreams for her life. "I live in an apartment even though I could own a condominium. I started out with only a cot and a table and chair, and that was it for the longest time. I never entertained because I didn't want anyone to see the way I lived," she said, with a hint of shame in her voice. "The only reason I have any furniture now is because my aunt died and my mother offered me her things. They're not my taste, but I don't have money to get what I really want—at least right now."

Amy also fears she could become self-indulgent if she had enough money to do what she'd like. "It's probably better that I don't have a surplus. I couldn't trust myself to spend it prudently."

Simone, too, admits that her pauper mentality has kept her from her true self, from doing what she really wants to do, which is to play the piano and go to graduate school for a science degree. She'd like money for a piano and lessons, and for tuition and books. And she'd really like to take a vacation —for the first time in many years.

Even as she reviews her desires, Simone admits that when it comes to money, "I'm afraid of blowing it all. But then I think of what I want, and the conflict starts again. My wants always exceed the money I have."

For Simone this is an old pattern. She voices her dreams and wishes and then feels there isn't enough money to make them happen. "I remember as a kid getting money and making a list of what I wanted. I'd feel frightened and excited at the same time. It was the kind of emotional rush you feel when you're in love. I remember a pair of sunglasses I bought and then lost before I fell out of love with them. It was awful."

Today Simone is practicing the principles and the Twelve Steps of Debtors Anonymous, and she is in private therapy to deal with her behavior patterns and the childhood issues around money. "The personal contact with other people in the program, working the steps with a friend, and sharing myself with others are the strong ties to recovery that are helping me become more responsible with the money I have."

Perpetual paupers—contrary to the stereotypical images of bag ladies pushing grocery carts or old women with $100,000 stowed under their mattresses—are women like you and me. They are found in every walk of life and are of every background and belief. The *pauper compulsion* is, first of all, a state of mind, fueled by a set of beliefs that drive the unwanted behavior.

Kelly, Nancy, and July know about the pauper mentality firsthand. They've agreed to share their stories.

Hand-to-mouth: Kelly's Story

"I used to think pauperism was the same as self-debting," said Kelly, a thirty-three-year-old administrative assistant. "But actually, it's not. Self-debting means I can't give to myself even though I may have the money to do so. Being a pauper means I *have to get rid* of my money."

At the same time, she *wants* money all the time. "I'm always scheming to get it. I take part-time jobs. And I sell things and wonder how much I'll make. Yet my husband and I make enough to live on."

While Kelly was growing up there was never enough food or money. Her whole childhood was hand-to-mouth. "There was *never* an excess," she said, stressing the negative. "When I was about five my mother became a single parent, and it was very shaming. I remember emptying my piggy bank for my mother." Even the *subject* of money has a shaming effect on Kelly—"whether you have it or you don't have it."

Today it is very hard for Kelly to distinguish between wants and needs. "For so long our family never had enough to pay bills. Now I have to pay and spend until there's nothing left." She can't buy groceries for just a week. She buys enough for twelve people. "If I have money I feel compelled to get rid of it, even if the purchases don't make sense. I also sabotage myself by spending the money that should be used for bills."

At one point Kelly had actually accumulated $500 in savings, but she couldn't leave it there. "I spent it all," she said, "on gas, electricity, phone. I took away from myself in order to pay bills."

Kelly's husband has what she calls complementary addictions. He is an overspender and a self-debtor. "I spend like mad, and he buys *me* things, but he can't spend money on himself. He seems to need my permission. For example, he might run out of shaving cream. He'll keep talking about needing it, but won't actually go to the store and buy it."

Kelly, her dark eyes intent as she spoke, said she is learning a lot about money and compulsive behavior during recovery. "It's taken me four years to understand the addiction process. I'm learning to take things back to the store, though it's a shaming experience for me. I'm also putting away some money just for me, and it feels good. I have $500 surplus in a checking account now, and it's going to stay there."

Kelly's recovery started in Narcotics Anonymous and is now continuing in Debtors Anonymous. "I found God in NA," she said with a lilt in her voice. "My spiritual life is now the most important thing in my life." But spirituality wasn't important in her family while she was growing up. Her family had what she called a religion-of-the-month. "Guilt, punishment, and perfectionism were the grounds. I was already shame-based at home, so this didn't help." But when she had a spiritual awakening in NA, she aligned her will with God's. "I can remember honestly hearing Him telling me gently that there is abundance for me. Today I really *feel* it."

Thread of Love: Nancy's Story

Nancy was born in Sioux Falls, South Dakota, and was adopted as an infant. She remembers two beliefs that guided her early life and influenced her as an adult. "First, I learned that I couldn't count on people—even my parents. I had to take care of myself. Once I learned that, I threw people out of my life. Second, I learned at church and in parochial school that the only perfect family was the Holy Family. So when I realized my family couldn't be perfect, I threw God out of my life too."

While growing up, Nancy also received a continuous message that you can't have what you want. "Like my mother, I was second best, and I always got second best. I hid out in school and did very well, but my mother always put down my grades. I remember buying candy to make myself feel better."

Nancy's spending and shopping began when she was about fifteen. "My mother was working then, so my refuges were the library, where it was quiet and orderly, and Fantal's department store because of its beautiful things. I believe I felt more like God's child in Fantal's than anywhere else. I felt prosperous when I was there. The bright, beautiful colors and shapes brought out my creativity."

But like most paupers, Nancy was influenced by her family patterns. She liked beautiful things, but she wasn't able to have them, so again she took refuge in school and attained bachelor's, master's, and doctoral degrees. Then "just like my mother," she went to work as a paralegal.

She married her first and only husband for the $10,000 he had at the time. She wanted him to take care of her, but it wasn't a marriage of love, and shortly afterward she began drinking. "In December of 1974, one day I woke up on the living room floor, drunk. I was thirty-four years old at the time. My father had died of alcoholism at the same age. Suddenly I

saw how I was repeating the pattern. Right then I stopped—
and went to my first AA meeting."

That same year, Nancy became restless for the truth about
her birth parents, and she traced her mother to Bloomington,
Minnesota. She learned that both her birth mother and her
adoptive mother had worked for the same attorney. "All my
abandonment issues came up the day I went to meet my natural mother. "We looked just alike. I knew I was her daughter."

They kept in contact for a while, but in recent years they
have not seen each other.

In the mid-seventies, Nancy and her husband moved to San
Diego. At the time they had $120,000 between them. By the
end of the decade they were divorced, and Nancy had $34,000
to start a new life. For a time she "pretended to be a realtor in
La Jolla," but that wasn't for her. She moved to the Hillcrest
area of San Diego, and "there I went into workaholism. I became cold and hard. By the time I hit Debtors Anonymous in
August 1990, I had no heart and no soul left. I was trying to
emulate my adoptive mother."

A true pauper, Nancy began ridding herself of her money by
binge-spending on clothes and running up $4,000 on her credit
cards. When she started attending DA meetings, she swung
the other way, stopped spending altogether, and went into
what she calls her miser phase. "I learned how to put a spending plan together, but after a few months, I stopped going to
meetings." She said she got what she needed and knew it was
time to move on. Nancy feels some of the DA principles are
too harsh for her. "I want gentle things in my life now."

Today God has a place in Nancy's life—for the first time
ever—and she said she feels His presence. "Now I take God
into my work, and I am more trusting, more sharing, and more
approachable than ever before. My creative energy has
soared. I see colors again and I feel my emotions. I'm more
myself and less an actor."

Now Nancy knows that God will provide, and He does. She
no longer has to rid herself of money and possessions in order
to repeat the past. "I believe God is leading me into my creativity more and more. I'm trusting Him to meet my needs,
and I'm taking small typing jobs as they come along, until I
know what I'm supposed to do next. I'm an artist at heart.

Right now I know I'd like to work in an art museum, and I want to train to become a docent."

And what about clothing for the new Nancy, who once longed to dress like the mannequins at Fantal's? "I buy my clothes at the Bargain Bungalow," she said, with a confident smile. "It's a resale shop a couple of blocks from where I live, and it has all the preppy fashions I like at the prices I can afford."

As for her career in the legal field, it's a thing of the past— along with drinking and binge-spending and a marriage that was never meant to be. "I withdrew from law, because when I work there I lose the thread of love in my life," the thread that carried Nancy from Minnesota to California and lifted her from pauperism to prosperity of the spirit.

Mixed Messages: July's Story

"My dad was a colonel in the Air Force," said July, an athletic woman with a warm smile and rapid-fire speech that demands you pay attention. I did, and I was drawn in by her enthusiasm and attentiveness.

"To us, his rank meant that we were better than others," she said. But at the same time, both her mother and father were practicing alcoholics. So the parental messages were mixed right from the start.

"I have an incredible history," said July, as she ran down the list of luxuries that permeated her early years. "For a time we lived in France in a chateau on twenty-six acres. The house had thirteen bedrooms and four bathrooms," she exclaimed, seemingly impressed all over again as she shared the story of her unusual upbringing.

The association with money and power was laid down early in July's life. "I remember a time when I was about seven or eight. I saw my folks in a fight with the landlord. I thought to myself, *we have money; this can't happen to us.*" The confusing dynamics in her parents' relationship with each other also caused her to receive mixed messages about money.

"Dad said we had enough. Mom said we didn't. It wasn't until three months ago that I learned the truth. They have close to $390,000 in assets and money that I'll come into one day. But when I think about it, it's really hard for me to get that for myself."

July has always pictured herself as not being capable, even though her parents never actually said anything negative to her. However, her father did most things involving money for her. "I took my checkbook to my dad for balancing. And when I was old enough to drive, he bought me a car. But I couldn't handle it by myself. When I got a flat tire I gave the car back to him. My folks also bought me a house," but that too became an overwhelming responsibility. "I remember being terrified to spend and to make decisions about money. I put only $37 on my credit card in two years! I was afraid of it."

As a young adult, July gradually buried her insecurities in drugs and alcohol until that overwhelmed her and she turned to AA for help. "But as soon as I got sober, my money addiction surfaced. I started ridding myself of all my money. I maxed out my credit cards. I bought things I didn't need or want. I couldn't keep up my house. I finally sold it to pay my debts, even though the message from home had been 'Don't sell property.'"

Even those experiences were not enough to stop her from pushing away the money she had through wild spending and charging. "I went right back into debt, this time up to seven or eight thousand dollars."

By then July knew her way around Twelve Step recovery programs, and she began attending meetings of Debtors Anonymous. She also met the man in her life around the same time and discovered that he has the same fear she has—the fear of not being enough. "We are both paupers. We have very mushy boundaries when it comes to money."

July, like Kelly, has "a real struggle" keeping more than $500 in savings at one time. "When it gets to that amount, something always happens. I notice that it's almost a relief when I get the balance below $500 again."

July also pushes money away by buying stuff that doesn't mean anything. "I have nothing to show for all the money I've spent. I also have self-debting issues. I can't make a commitment to myself."

Through the recovery, however, she has made a significant personal commitment, and returned to sports. "I'm now involved in triathalon competitions: swimming, biking, and running. And this requires spending some money. There's a hefty entry fee that I'm now willing to pay, and I've also invested in an expensive camera for my career."

July took a moment to talk about her spiritual life. She said that when she entered her first recovery program she had "a spurt of enormous spiritual growth, but then it slowed down. I think I was afraid of becoming a self-help junkie," she said, laughing. "But now I'm beginning to feel spiritually flabby. I'm losing my tone. I know what it's like to surrender to a higher power—I did that in my other program. I knew when I couldn't fight it alone anymore. Okay, I told myself, the universe wins!"

July admits that she "leans toward a rational view" of something bigger than herself. "I know there's a power greater than I am. However, at this point in my life, it's a power I don't understand. But I do respect it."

Then pausing for a moment, she said slowly, "Yeah, I'd like to have a spiritual life again. It was a reality for me at one time."

Taking Inventory

Women who are perpetual paupers answer "often" or "very often" to many of these statements.

1. I push money away.

2. I feel relieved when I have to spend money.

3. I have a difficult time keeping money in a savings account.

4. I keep myself on the edge financially.

5. I'm scared that I won't be able to handle money responsibly.

6. I am uncomfortable with large sums of money.

7. I find a way to spend or give away my money.

8. I spend money set aside for bills on items I don't need or want.

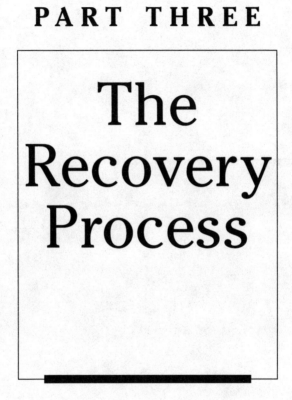

PART THREE

The
Recovery
Process

11

Telling and Receiving the Truth

In 1978 I made an appointment with a counselor I had met some years before while doing research for one of my books. I had been impressed by his compassion, his professionalism, and most important to me at the time, his empathy for troubled marriages.

I remember sitting in his office waiting room the afternoon of my first session, leafing through a magazine as my right leg bounced nervously atop my left knee. "Get in, get a few tips, and get out," I told myself. I had no intention of entering long-term therapy. I honestly believed the solution to my problems could be contained on a recipe card.

Wisely the counselor encouraged me to share my story. After I rushed through the chronology of events and behaviors, I sat back in my chair and waited for him to tell me what to *do*.

"How do you feel about all this?" he asked, giving special emphasis to the word *feel*.

"Feel? What do you mean how do I feel?" I asked, repeating his question with a touch of annoyance.

"I'm wondering what it feels like," he persisted, "to be treated in such an uncaring way, to be in debt, to be neglected, to be set aside for another woman."

"I don't know," I said, dumbfounded. "Is it important to know how I feel? No one's ever asked me how I felt about anything in my whole life. I've just tried to do what's right, and I hoped you'd tell me the right thing to do now."

THE TRUTH ABOUT ME

I'll never forget that experience. It was the day I became acquainted with my emotional self. I needed some help putting my feelings into words, but before I left the counseling office, I was able to say that I felt *hurt, sad,* and *disappointed.* It was a start. Admitting those feelings led to uncovering deeper levels of emotion, and over time I was finally able to express the most frightening feelings of all—guilt, anger, and ultimately rage.

I'm sharing this here because it demonstrates to me in a very personal way the power of *telling the truth as we experience it—not simply as we know it.* I knew a lot of information. I had even written a book about women and money and another about communication in marriage. But they were of little benefit to me during my crisis because I was in so much emotional pain.

That first session of private therapy, however, opened a door within that had been closed and locked most of my life. The sad part is I didn't even know there was anything under lock and key. I had lived my life from the perspective of *doing.*

During the months in therapy, however, I began to see tiny glimpses of a side of life I had never known. I began to *feel.* Pain. Sadness. Anger. I was coming alive. Choices and options seemed available for the first time. It was okay for me to tell my husband no, that I would not co-sign for another loan. It was all right to say I felt angry and hurt when he walked out on a conversation with me.

I also noticed that whenever I was able to express my emotions honestly, I would feel better emotionally immediately. Gradually I felt a change in my physical health as well. I had fewer headaches, stomach cramps, and colon spasms and less upper back pain. And the more I voiced my feelings, the less power my thoughts had. I became more playful, more child-like, more available to people and to life.

This process of self-discovery reminded me of a time I took my sewing machine apart and put it back together again. I had gone after a thread that was jamming the system. I uncovered one part at a time and set it aside in an orderly way until I got to the thread. Then I plucked it out, tossed it away, and slowly and carefully put the pieces back together. Finally, I turned on the machine and sewed a few test stitches. It worked!

In a similar way, I had begun taking myself apart, going after the thread of truth that I knew was caught on some interior part of me. As I slowly and methodically dismantled beliefs and barriers that had jammed my system, I gained a new sense of myself. I paid close attention to each part. I was beginning to learn the truth about myself, my past, my pain, and the role I played in becoming a woman in debt.

THE TRUTH ABOUT GOD

As I continued my search, I also became acutely aware of a deep void at the center of my life—a hole that had been there all along, but that I was just beginning to notice. I was to discover, in the months and years ahead, that this missing element was the truth about God.

Knowing the truth about myself meant nothing without knowing the truth about God. I learned this in December 1982, following a long spiritual journey that took me from Catholicism to Religious Science and down several paths in between. I attended church services, lectures, workshops, and Bible studies. I read books, listened to tapes, and prayed the best way I knew.

Then one morning after returning from a walk along the ocean near my home in San Diego, I found the thread of truth I had been searching for all my life without knowing it: Jesus Christ. As I cried out to God in confusion and despair over a troubled second marriage, chaotic finances, and hurting children, I collapsed on the grass in a heap. I realized then that I knew a lot *about* God, but I didn't really *know* Him in a personal way—in a way that would make a difference in my life.

That morning through the saving grace of Jesus Christ, God met me exactly where I was. He impressed on my spirit that day the words from Scripture that I had read dozens of times before: "I am the way, the truth, and the life. No one comes to the Father except through Me" (John 14:6).

Suddenly I saw the *truth* of those words—for me. I needed a Savior. I needed and wanted the assurance of salvation, forgiveness, and eternal life that only Jesus Christ can provide. The experience was real. It was life-changing. It was deeply personal.

Until that moment, I had seen Jesus as a great teacher, the son of God, a miracle-worker, a healer. But I did not know Him as *my* Lord and Savior. I had never fully embraced the truth that He died for *me* so that *my* sins could be forgiven and so that *I* could have life everlasting.

THE TRUTH ABOUT EVERYONE

In the years since, I have seen that without God's truth we cannot fully experience the truth about ourselves in any meaningful and lasting way. We need God's wisdom and grace and mercy as we make a commitment to end our compulsive cycles with money.

Without exception I have seen the women in debt with whom I've talked and prayed make a dramatic turn in their recovery processes when they commit themselves and their situations to God.

For many women this is one of the most difficult decisions they will ever make. Many of them were spiritually abused as children by parents who used the authority of God to frighten and diminish them. Others were raised in homes where legalism and religious doctrine were more important than the relationship between the child and God. And still others were emotionally or sexually abused by a religious representative, such as a minister, priest, or Sunday school teacher.

For many God became synonymous with religion, ritual, rules, and regulations that did not allow for the natural spontaneity and curiosity that are a part of being a child. Somewhere in that child's growing-up process, the God of love and forgiveness and grace gave way to an authority figure of harsh judgment and punishment.

In my own life, I spent years trying to please a presence I did not know or understand. I attended church most of my life, yet I did not have any sense of comfort or encouragement from the God I tried to worship.

I found Him, instead, on a grassy knoll above the Pacific Ocean that December morning when I was at the very bottom of myself. It was a simple visitation by a loving God who called me to Himself for the healing I had longed for. For me that spot will always be holy ground, and San Diego will always be God's promised land, for it was there that I experienced a new beginning.

I believe that the truth about each one of us is that we have a deep hunger for the fellowship and forgiveness of God. Women in debt who have been forgiven by husbands, children, parents, and co-workers claim even that is not enough. They are tormented by their wrongdoing until they know with certainty that God has forgiven them. I don't know any way to offer that assurance outside of the saving grace of Jesus Christ.

WHAT THE TRUTH MEANS IN YOUR LIFE TODAY

Will your life be totally free of pain once you make that commitment? Are you doomed to a life of pain if you don't make it? The answer to both questions is no. *God meets us where we are.*

If we come to Him in pain, and most people do, He guides us as we walk toward the pain, comforts us while we're in it, and provides the grace and direction we need to move through it. In *The Living Bible,* we are reminded to "let him have all your worries and cares, for he is always thinking about you and watching everything that concerns you" (1 Pet. 5:7).

How does a woman in debt begin to tell the truth about herself and learn the truth about God? There are no set rules, religious tracts, Bible verses, or courses of action that are right for everyone. That would be a form of legalism and ritual we are trying to avoid.

But I do believe there is a necessary first step to take in order to get the process going. It starts with *willingness*—being *willing* to tell and receive the truth. If even being willing is too much for you at this point, then you can start with *being willing* to *become willing.* God will meet you there and provide the guidance and grace for what comes next.

It is my deep conviction that no lasting recovery can occur

unless and until we become willing to take action and receive support. Even the first step of the Twelve Step programs, admitting one's powerlessness over one's life and one's addiction, may be too scary for you at this time. But if you are *willing to become willing,* you will have opened the door to the truth about yourself and your situation, the truth about God, and the truth about the importance of both. God will lead you from there.

In Proverbs 3:6 we are advised, "In all your ways acknowledge Him, and He shall direct your paths." I can think of no better words for a hungry heart. If you are ready to take that important first step, stop for a moment now and tell God in your own words that you are willing—or at the very least that you are willing to become willing—to tell and receive the truth.

ASKING FOR HELP

You may have identified with many of the women in debt you read about in this book. You may have related to their drive to shop or gamble or overspend or to enable others to use money compulsively. You may also be wondering how to go about changing the course of your addictive behavior once you are willing to change. How can you experience and apply the truths you are discovering?

Dr. Carla Perez, a psychiatrist in San Francisco who has worked with compulsive spenders and shoppers, claims: "You have to start to attack the problem by interrupting either the trigger or the opportunity. Resolving the emotional conflicts that cause the addiction can take a very long time. But while you're working on the emotional trigger, you can take practical steps to interrupt the opportunity."[1]

I agree. But I also believe that the practical steps you take need to be rooted in spirituality if they are to have any permanent value. To tell a woman to buy only what she needs, or to go to a movie instead of a gambling casino, or to cut up her credit cards is not a solution. It may work for a time, but when the compulsive urge comes over her again or when the pain in her life becomes severe, she will overspend, gamble, or shop, regardless of her commitment to do otherwise.

The important first step in committing to any form of recovery is admitting you have a problem, acknowledging that you're powerless to recover on your own, and then asking God to lead you to the program and the support system that is best for you.

That might include a number of options: private therapy with a counselor who specializes in addictive behaviors, particularly issues with money; group therapy with other women in debt; or one of the Twelve Step support programs listed in the Supplementary Resources at the back of this book.

Asking for help means taking some action on your behalf. If you are not ready to attend a meeting or find a counselor, you might continue reading. Perhaps this is your first book on money addiction. You may wish to read others, some of which I've listed in the Appendix. Or you may reach out for telephone help through a prayer ministry, a crisis hot-line, or simply a trusted friend to share your feelings with.

If you do decide to commit to Debtors Anonymous or another program or to enter long-term therapy, be sure that you give each experience enough time to work. You did not become a woman in debt overnight, and you will not get out of it overnight.

Asking for help implies a level of trust that requires you to let go of your controlling behavior and surrender to a process of recovery that will include the guiding influence and support of another person or a group. If you are a Christian, I encourage you to look for a Christian counselor, someone who understands and acknowledges that Jesus Christ is the center of your life.

If you are not a Christian, but you do believe in God and practice a spiritual discipline, then I encourage you to choose a therapist who will be respectful and sympathetic to your views and goals, and one who is familiar with the destructive cycle you want to break.

Putting herself in the care of another human being can be a very frightening experience for a woman who already feels out of control in her life. But give yourself and your counselor a chance. Take a deep breath and whisper a prayer to God as you understand Him right now, and then *trust*. The Bible says that God knows our every need even before we ask Him. What a comforting thought. He will lead us in the paths we must go, if we but ask.

You may also be wondering *why* it is important to ask for help. It's important because you've already tried to do it on your own and that didn't work. You've already made a million promises you didn't keep, and you have already borrowed, loaned, spent, charged, or gambled your way into debt time and again.

If you had a cavity you wouldn't try to fill your tooth yourself. If you needed a new set of brakes for your car, chances are you would not attempt to install them yourself. So why struggle alone with something as important as your life? Help is out there. Ask and you will receive.

You may be one who already has a solid belief in God and a loving relationship with Him. You may feel that is all you need. You and God will handle this alone, thank you very much! This point of view, however, breeds isolation, and isolation tends to foster denial. Without support from others, we slip back into our old ways. We become unwilling and, eventually, unable to see what is really going on.

Beyond that, the God-and-me approach to life is not realistic. Humans are social as well as spiritual beings. God intended us to relate to one another. Frequently, He speaks to us through other people. Assume that your situation is worse than you can see or imagine it to be. Ask for help even if you don't think you need it. At the very least, you will receive encouragement for the progress you are making. And at the very most, you will discover how needy you are and will welcome the help that is available.

12

It's Not About Money After All

One of the great discoveries of women recovering from financial debt is the fact that the *real* issues they face are not about money after all. Spending plans, repayment of debts, earning, saving, and managing money—essential as they are to reversing the destructive behaviors of gambling, under-earning, or shopping—are not the most important aspects of recovery.

True recovery is about entrusting our lives and our situations to God. It's about getting ourselves right spiritually and emotionally so we can use the practical tools in a God-directed way. It's about laying up treasures in heaven, not on earth, "for where your treasure is, there will your heart be also" (Matt. 6:21).

The pressing need today is not for more women of independent means or for more intelligent, creative, or assertive women. The pressing need today is for women of spiritual substance, women willing to make the inward journey to the deep treasures of the spirit.

Prayer, the life and breath of the spiritual life, is undoubtedly the means to that goal. A life without prayer is a life without power.

Richard Foster, author of *Celebration of Discipline,* says that prayer "brings us into the deepest and highest work of the human spirit. Real prayer is life creating and life changing."[1]

It is through prayer and meditation that we experience the quieting presence of God, commune with Him on a personal level, and hear His guidance. If we are committed to being transformed, we will be committed to prayer. Prayer is also the gateway to the spiritual disciplines—the paths by which we enter the life of the spirit. In this chapter, we will be looking at seven disciplines and how we can practice them as we move forward in our spiritual recovery.

Whenever we embark on a new journey, we may be tempted to follow the map so closely that we miss the lovely surprises God has put in our itinerary. He may encourage us to pluck a daisy from the side of the road or contemplate a waterfall on a distant mountain. Be ready for these serendipitous delights. Hold your map loosely!

Unknowingly we may also turn the suggestions and invitations here into laws, and then hold ourselves and others accountable to these standards. But we can rest assured that God will help us if that happens, for He has promised He will never leave us nor forsake us. He asks that we lean on His understanding, not our own: "I will instruct you and teach you in the way you should go; I will guide you with My eye" (Ps. 32:8).

RECOVERING FROM SPIRITUAL BANKRUPTCY

Many hurting women have no idea how spiritually bankrupt they are. They cannot even imagine a life without struggle. But the very moment we declare our willingness to recover from spiritual bankruptcy, we enter the healing process. "Come to Me, all you who labor and are heavy laden, and I will give you rest" (Matt. 11:28).

What a comforting promise! What we carried for so long will now be God's. Think of it. God will close the old account and open a new one in partnership with Him—a spiritual bank account that deals in the currency of seven spiritual disciplines: study, surrender, service, solitude, simplicity, solvency, and serenity. Many of the disciplines are familiar. We have read about them, wrestled with them in our own lives, even practiced them from time to time.

Some of us may have held back, assuming they are too challenging or time-consuming for women who must care for families, raise children, tend homes, or work in the marketplace. Others may have admired them from afar, assigning them to mystics and contemplatives who spend their lives in prayer and fasting. On the contrary, the disciplines of the spiritual life are God's gifts to every woman. In fact it is on the ordinary streets of life that He does His most transforming work.

I believe that more than ever before, our world needs women who not only practice the disciplines but embrace them, not as an expression of legalism, but as an affirmation of a spirit who truly knows God as her source, her support, her very supply. I hope you choose to be among them.

THE DISCIPLINE OF STUDY

What *study* means

I believe the most important discipline we can commit to in the initial phase of recovery is the *discipline of study*. The apostle Paul in his letter to the Romans says transformation comes about through the renewing of the mind (see Rom. 12:2).

Those of us who have suffered from spiritual abuse, addictions, and compulsive behavior around money need our minds renewed and transformed. Attitudes of hopelessness, negative thinking, and low self-esteem have kept many of us from God's guidance. A season of committed study can open the path to His transforming grace and lead to the next discipline, surrender.

To study is to learn by examining, analyzing, investigating, reading and thinking, concentrating, and understanding a piece of written work such as a book or journal. We might also study an animal, a flower, a rock, a sunset. As we study and think, we form thoughts about the object. As a body of knowledge and perceptions take root in our minds, they become the basis for our actions. We are reminded in Proverbs 23:7 that as we think, so we are.

It is up to us, then, to choose with care the material we study and reflect on. As Paul reminds us, "Whatever is true, whatever is noble, whatever is right, whatever is pure, whatever is lovely, whatever is admirable . . . think about such things" (Phil. 4:8 NIV).

How to practice *studying* in your life today

To me the most inspiring and useful opportunity for study is the Bible. It is a handbook for life, providing the most complete selection of all that is true, noble, right, pure, lovely, and admirable—from the creation of life to the revelation of life to come.

There is a difference, however, between *studying* the Bible and reading it for inspiration and comfort. Studying is searching a passage for its meaning, concentrating on a word or phrase until you see the truth of it, discovering the intention of the author, and finding and holding fast to God's message. Studying is applying your mind. It is a task and function of the intellect. Studying is working.

Reading for inspiration and devotion has more to do with basking in the warm glow of God's promises and allowing your spirit to meditate on the things of God for strength and provision.

Other objects of study might include reference books, such as dictionaries and encyclopedias, anthologies on topics of interest, fiction that uplifts and inspires, and nonfiction that instructs, encourages, and provides practical application of a set of instructions or principles that will help us to lead a more worthwhile life.

We can apply the discipline of study to our issues with money as well. If we want to create a spending plan that works or talk with our creditors, or make informed choices about a job search, a bank account, or an interview, we will need to study these things. New ways of responding to old patterns will not simply emerge fully perfected. They must be pulled down from the shelf, examined, and analyzed.

This discipline also requires a willingness to make ourselves the object of our study, so that we might really see our patterns and prejudices, our beliefs and boundaries. Without attending to ourselves, we run the risk of continuing down the same paths while expecting different results.

For some of us the discipline of study may include returning to school for a college degree in order to begin a new profession or to pursue an interest in a foreign language, in nature and the wilderness, or in travel or real estate or medicine. Studying involves a deep conviction and commitment to personal renewal. It is more than the mere reading of a book or contemplation of our lives or the creation around us. Studying is aligning with the truth and trusting that, as God promised through Jesus, "the truth will set you free" (John 8:32 NIV). Once we know the truth of God's word, we can move into the next discipline—*surrender*—without hesitation.

THE DISCIPLINE OF SURRENDER

What *surrender* means

Women who are familiar with Twelve Step recovery programs know the importance of the third step: "Made a decision to turn our wills and our lives over to the care of God as we understood Him."[2]

No lasting transformation can occur in our lives without giving control to a power greater than we are. And yet no discipline has been more abused by individuals, families, schools, and religious leaders.

Parents demand that children submit to their authority. Warring nations demand surrender of the weaker party to the stronger party or that wrong surrender to right. Surrender has a bad reputation. In some circles, it suggests a form of bondage, a giving away of all that is valuable and dear and unique to the individual.

And no wonder. Many of us have been forced to surrender, made to submit, humiliated into subordination as children, wives, employees, even friends.

The discipline of surrender, however, has nothing to do with bondage. It is an expression of freedom. Giving up is releasing to God for His safekeeping those people and situations we have no control over anyway. Surrender releases us from carrying the burden of the process as well as the results. We can then walk in freedom, knowing with absolute certainty that the God of the universe, the One who knows all things, who is for all time, will bring about in our lives what is right and good and pure and just, not only in the financial realm, but in every area of our lives as well.

How to practice *surrender* in your life today

The discipline of surrender liberates us. But it also challenges us to express it in accordance with God's will. The danger is in overspiritualizing it, and thus missing its great gifts. Surrender must never be used to manipulate others or to gain spiritual authority over them. The it's-out-of-my-hands-so-don't-expect-anything-from-me mentality has no place in this discipline.

God-directed surrender suggests that we first submit to His authority and will for our lives. It can be as simple as declaring your willingness in prayer when you awaken in the morning. You might say something as simple as the following:

> *God, today I surrender my whole self to you, everything I think and say and do. Cause me to do your will and to be a blessing to myself and to everyone I come in contact with today.*

After we start our day by surrendering to God in prayer, we will be ready to surrender to our families. That means being available, making our presence known and felt, listening and caring, and making it clear that each person matters.

As we move from home to community, we will surely find opportunities to surrender to neighbors and friends, to co-workers, and to those who are downtrodden, sick, and alone, as well as to those who live on the fringes of society. Is there a way we can surrender something useful of our own to someone in need? Even a prized possession, perhaps? Could we surrender a portion of our time to pray with the sick? To shop for the elderly? To help someone move into a new home? To provide food for the hungry?

And we must not forget our place in the world at large, our responsibility to surrender self-centered needs for the greater good of our planet, whether through wilderness conservation, animal protection, or curbing our use of precious natural resources. Those of us who have held ourselves or others hostage through money can surrender our financial obsessions and then reach out to others with the same needs.

In fact we cannot fully practice the discipline of surrender without combining it with service. The two work together. Surrender without service is akin to telling a hungry woman you'll pray for her without first giving her some bread. And service without true surrender is a work of the flesh and will most certainly lead to burnout.

If our first act of surrender each day is to God Himself, then we can proceed, confident that He will direct us to the places and people He has planned for us to serve.

THE DISCIPLINE OF SERVICE

What *service* means

Women who are recovering from codependence and addictive behavior are understandably wary when it comes to the discipline of service. They may see it as the doormat discipline because they have, for so long, allowed others to wipe their shoes on them. But true service is far from that. Service that springs from the heart and soul is a gift of self.

Serving is giving something of yourself to another—whether money, material goods, a listening ear, a prayer, a portion of time, a talent, or a treasure. One who serves from the spirit knows when to say yes and when to say no. She knows what part is hers and what part belongs to another because she lives with one eye and ear attuned to the natural realm and one eye and ear fixed on the spiritual, the source of guidance.

How to practice *service* in your life today

In practicing the discipline of service we must again turn to God for direction through prayer and meditation. True service is not self-serving. It is self-giving. And most importantly, it is God-directed.

For many years I was unclear about this discipline. I knew the value of sharing my time and talent with others—from Scout leader to classroom aid, from volunteer at a crisis center to Sunday school teacher. But I had no sense of balance.

Like everything else in my life I served compulsively, and I had a lot of "should" attached to it.

I did not see that true service is rooted in the heart, not in the hands. I assumed that every call to serve was a call on my life. I measured my worth by the amount of time and work I donated each month, until I nearly collapsed from burnout. Then guilt set in. It did not occur to me to pray about each situation before committing to it—that is, until one healing week while teaching a writing course at a camp in the Sierra Mountains.

I laid out my pain and conflict before God one day while walking in the woods. His response was swift and clear. He had called me *to write* and *to teach* and *to pray*, according to His will for me, not according to my agenda. I can still recall the incredible rush of relief I felt the moment I took in this clear and direct message.

He then confirmed His words through Scripture and through other people I spoke with during the week. I came to realize that week that I could contribute to animal protection, homeless children, resource conservation, wildlife awareness, and women in debt—subjects I feel passionately about—by writing books about them. And I was to pray for the people He directed me to and in the way He led me. That was another liberating experience. I didn't have to make the decisions about what to do or who to spend time with or which writing projects to accept or reject. My work life was transformed that week, and I've been at peace about it ever since.

That same clarity is available to each one of us. When our service is God-directed there will be no struggle. We will not need to prove our worth, earn awards, make our mark, achieve recognition, or drive ourselves to exhaustion. What is done in secret will be rewarded in heaven—where it matters.

THE DISCIPLINE OF SILENCE

What *silence* means

Most people think of *silence* as the absence of sound, just as the dictionary defines the word. But as a spiritual discipline,

...s to shopping and overspending and abusing credit
... But what a great gust of cleansing wind it could be, as
...if we were to greet it with enthusiasm.

...d to those who have found their worth through gambling
...nabling others to go into debt, the discipline of simplic-
...fers the opportunity to find our worth on the inside in-
... of on the outside.

...women who push money away through self-debt, under-
...ng, and pauperism, a life of simplicity can restore a sense
...gnity and purpose and balance. We can choose to live our
...free of materialism, free of the need to *prove* our value by
...ing ourselves even the necessities. As the familiar Shaker
...n reminds us, "It's a gift to be simple, It's a gift to be free.
... gift to come down where we ought to be."³

...many women in debt, coming down to where they ought
... would be a gift indeed. Coming down from fantasy to
...ty, from grandiosity to sincerity, from dishonesty to hon-
...where they can live in both prudence and plenty.

...nplicity is not austerity, which renounces the things of
...vorld. Instead, it puts those things in proper perspective.
...licity encourages us to be well, look well, feel well, and
...ell without making a statement about it. Simplicity allows
... drive an old car because we want to, not because we
...to. Or to drive a new car because we want to, not be-
...e we have to. Like the apostle Paul, we can be content in
...ty or in want, because simplicity, like all the disciplines,
...is on the inside. When we are simple within, we are free
...out.

...mplicity," says Richard Foster, "sets us free to receive
...rovision of God as a gift that is not ours to keep, and that
...be freely shared with others."⁴

...to practice *simplicity* in your life today

...en the desire for a simple lifestyle, however, cannot take
...edence over our relationship with God or it too can be-
... an addiction! Simplicity means taking our hands off the
...rols and depending on God, as do the birds of the air and
...lies of the field.

...acticing simplicity involves trust and prudence. For
...en in debt, this may be a challenging step that requires

silence is much more than an absence. It is also a presence—
God's presence in quiet communion with our presence.

Simply refraining from speaking, however, is to miss the gift
of wisdom that God has for those who listen for His voice in
the silence.

In returning and rest you shall be saved. (Isa. 30:15)

Be still, and know that I am God. (Ps. 46:10)

I will lead them in paths they have not known. (Isa. 42:16)

Yet despite these encouraging words, most of us are so fearful
of being silent that we carry around our familiar blanket of
noise wherever we go. We depend on the hum of radios and
tape decks in our cars, our CD players, televisions and video
players in our homes, and portable audio cassettes strapped
to our heads and waists as we walk or run.

For many of us silence is a fearful thing, an intruder. Perhaps as a little girl you were punished with silence. If you did
a bad thing, your parents gave you the silent treatment, or
you were sent to your room to stay there in silence, or you
were told to hush or keep your mouth shut.

Or if you come from a large, noisy household, you may have
longed for a few moments of silence but never got them. Or
perhaps you craved a time of solitude under a tree, or by a
river bank, or in a secret hideaway, where you could think and
dream and write or listen to the birds or pray.

As an adult it may be painful for you to even consider carv-
ing out a time of silence. You may not know what to do with it
or how to benefit from it. The moment you sit down with
yourself and your thoughts, you might suddenly remember a
letter you must write, a load of clothes that needs pressing, a
stack of lessons that need correcting, a pile of bills that need
paying.

Silence is not an easy discipline to embrace. We talk about
it, think of it, and wish for it, but rarely do we experience it.
Entering silence requires a step of faith, a commitment to nur-
ture ourselves, a willingness to stop the noise and see what's
on the other side. It also requires that we practice being

alone, moving into a space of solitude, where we can listen and hear and experience the comfort and power of God within us.

Agnes Sanford, a pioneer in the prayer and healing movement in the Christian church, said she could never have done the work the Lord gave her to do without regular, committed times of silence.

And Susanna Wesley, mother of nineteen children—among them John, the founder of Methodism, and Charles, a famous hymn writer—spent two hours a day in silence and prayer, and this was in the 1700s, long before microwave ovens and clothes dryers and day-care.

It is one thing to be inspired by the practice of others, and quite another to be motivated for ourselves. All of the disciplines require courage and commitment, but perhaps silence and solitude more than any others. We depend on words. To be without them can make us feel defenseless. But silence calls us to stop the self-talk, the mindless head chatter, the rational thinking, the planning, and the manipulation that take up so much of our lives.

We can practice. And when our ideas and dreams demand a hearing, when guilt, worry, and doubt compete for attention, and when problems shout for a solution, we can whisper, "Hush. I'm waiting on God. In quietness and trust is my salvation."

And if we persist, oh, the treasures of the spirit that we will receive. Pretense and apology will disappear. Familiar burdens will become unimportant. Our need to control people and events will give way to the steadying hand of God. And we will begin to let go of our stockpile of jealousy, anger, fear, pride, and bitterness.

Wisely the writer of Ecclesiastes says there is "a time to keep silent and a time to speak." Those of us who wish to practice the discipline of silence will heed those words.

How to practice *silence* in your life today

How do we find quiet in a noisy world? How do we get *there* from *here?* First, we can take hold of small swatches of time as they appear. Find a place, or create one, where you can be alone and enter silence. One woman I know has "lunch with

the Lord." She brings her food in a brown bag and under a tree near her office where she eats and re in her journal, or simply sits in silence for the h each day.

Next, we can choose a time and put it on the c any other engagement. You might commit one month to a silent retreat when you go away phys park, a church or a temple, the woods or the sea yourself in silence. You might consider fasting a time each week and using that time to commune w and God in silence.

Small pockets of inner silence are also possible the morning as we awaken and lie quietly in our last thing at night before dropping off to sleep.

During the day we can enter inner silence while line at the post office or the bank or sitting in a do ing room. Even with the noise of others around learn to turn our spiritual ears to the things of Go have experienced this inner silence, the world car ily disrupt us again. We know what it is to be still a God.

And, oh, what fruit the tree of silence bears! We v as our inner persons are changed and healed of speak everything that is on our minds, of the desir record straight, of the compulsion to tell others and how to behave.

We will suddenly notice that we have the ability t financial and other problems without struggle. L guidance will be there at the precise moments we We will experience the release of creative expressic haps most importantly, an abiding sense of trust ness of God's presence at *all* times.

THE DISCIPLINE OF SIMPLICITY

What *simplicity* means

Simplicity is an absence of ornament, of show an it is freedom from useless accessories. What an discipline this could be for those of us who have

the prayer and support and wisdom of caring people before and after we make decisions about how to spend or save or invest our money.

A simpler life includes learning how to make wise choices about our clothing and transportation and housing needs. Do you really need fifteen pairs of shoes? Can you enjoy your clothing for several seasons, rather than answering the call to every fashion trend that comes along? Are you willing to live in a modest dwelling that is affordable and comfortable, rather than a showplace that drains your earnings each month?

Simplicity encourages us to modify our diets, to embrace simple, nourishing foods that we can prepare at home and share with others, instead of cramming fast foods into our mouths while we drive or read the paper or finish a report at work.

The simple life also embraces a caring and consciousness about the earth and its resources. If you are a meat-eater, perhaps you could experiment with a few vegetarian meals each week. If you use paper goods, you may want to consider replacing them with washable, recyclable materials.

Simplifying could mean clearing out the physical and emotional clutter in our lives—from old magazines to old friends who no longer nourish us. Do we really need to subscribe to every publication that interests us? Must we have our own washer and dryer, video player, and a television in every room? Or could we take advantage of these items and services available through community resources, such as the public library and neighborhood laundry?

How liberating it can be to use something without owning it. Wouldn't it be lovely to be free of dusting items we don't need, fixing things that continue to break, replacing equipment that wears out?

My husband and I have only recently discovered this truth for ourselves. We live in a wonderful apartment near the ocean in San Diego. The location is ideal for our lifestyle, and the rooms are generous in size. We have a delightful public park nearby, and we can walk or run along the beach every day if we wish. The post office, library, church, grocery store, and other businesses are all within a short drive or walk.

Yet, during the eleven years we've lived here, we've both

had the nagging thought that we *should* own our own place. We had fallen into the trap of thinking that rent is a poor use of our money. We don't have the tax advantages that property owners have, no equity is building, and on and on.

During our healing process with money issues, however, we both realized that we were bowing to the pressures of the American *should* system.

If we are pleased by this place, if it meets our needs and desires and satisfies the criteria we have for a home, then it is a *good* investment, regardless of what anyone else thinks. And we have also come to realize the distinct advantage of being able to call the manager for a plumbing or electrical repair or to pick up our mail while we are away. This year we have embraced our home anew. I honestly feel I would enjoy living here for the rest of my life.

The discipline of simplicity can also be applied to your inner life. For example, you could streamline your prayers so that God does more of the talking and you do more listening! You could also heed His command to pray without ceasing by making your life a prayer chain, each link connected by short one-line prayers of praise, and petition throughout the day: "Lord, watch over me in the meeting today." "Lord, thank you for that delicious lunch." "God, I need your strength tonight." "Father God, I know that you are providing for my every need."

Simplicity: the discipline that brings us down to where we ought to be so we can move into a solvent lifestyle.

SOLVENCY

What *solvency* means

Solvency—the ability to pay all that one owes—is the goal of all women in debt who desire real freedom. But there remains for many of us a great gap between the desire and the reality. That is when Twelve Step programs and other support groups can be so helpful. In one of these meetings, you can share your tragedies and your triumphs and be heard, understood, and loved.

The discipline of solvency challenges us to discover our

needs and wants, to bring them into perspective in terms of what is real and true in our lives, such as earnings, the season of our lives, the status of our households and dependent family members, and then to bring all of this before God for His guidance and blessing.

How to practice *solvency* in your life today

Solvency is not a discipline that a woman in debt can practice without support. What has taken a lifetime to dismantle cannot be restored through sheer willpower.

But we can take the initial steps that prepare us for the support of others by confronting our patterns with money. I know of no better avenue than Debtors Anonymous for this first step toward living a solvent life. There you will receive the practical guidance and encouragement you'll need to create a spending plan, talk to your creditors, and make amends to those you've hurt financially. You will also receive the emotional and spiritual support you'll need to tackle the deeper issues that are the true cause of your financial compulsions.

I believe solvency and simplicity are closely connected. Simplicity provides a solid foundation on which solvency can be practiced. When a woman in debt embraces simplicity she says to herself and others that she is committed to freeing herself of the tangles of the world. And when that commitment takes place deep within her, she will begin to practice solvency almost without realizing it.

Solvency, like the other disciplines, is "an inside job," as one woman observed. What occurs in the spiritual realm will show up in the natural realm as soon as a woman commits to living her life free of debt. Such women earn, save, share, spend, and invest out of a deep conviction, based on God's guidance, of what is right and true and just.

Practicing solvency in our lives also includes a willingness to learn all we can about practical financial matters that affect our everyday affairs. It means we take an interest in managing checking accounts, handling cash in responsible ways, planning for future needs and wants, setting aside funds for emergencies, investments, vacations, and retirement.

It includes praying for guidance about who to talk to, which seminars to attend, what books to read and tapes to listen to.

The discipline of solvency is the outworking of an inward commitment to become good stewards of the resources God provides.

A solvent lifestyle, then, results in a deep peace that paves the way for a life of serenity.

SERENITY

What *serenity* means

Serenity is a state of calm, of peacefulness, of a deep inner knowledge that all is well. This is the plane of life that women in recovery most desire. Thankfully serenity is not tied to any one practice or any one area of life. It is, instead, a spiritual discipline that brings about a state of total well-being as a woman comes to rest in God. To be serene is to be accepting, to hold life, self, and other people with an open hand instead of a clenched fist.

How to practice *serenity* in your life today

I cannot think of a better way to practice serenity than to live the words of the Serenity Prayer:

God, grant me the serenity
to accept the things I cannot change,
courage to change the things I can,
and wisdom to know the difference.[5]

Individuals who live these words no longer lean on themselves or the things of the world. They know that their personal power is limited and that they are effective only to the extent that God empowers them. They do not waste time trying to figure out what to do, what to say, or how to respond. They go to God *first*. And they ask for the power they need to accept whatever comes at them that they cannot change. Then they ask for the courage to change what they can. This takes some doing because it implies that they will be given the knowledge of what they can change, and they must then do it. Finally, and most importantly, they seek the wisdom they need to know the difference between the two. Without wisdom their serenity would be jeopardized. In all cases, they come before God, leaning on His power and understanding, not on their own. And in so doing they release the results to Him, as well, further ensuring their serenity and the right and just outworking of God in the lives of those around them. What freedom!

STREAMS IN THE DESERT

As we take up the spiritual journey, we can turn to the disciplines, like streams in a desert, to refresh our spirits when we feel dry and to guide us when we feel lost. And for those times when we feel strong and sure-footed, the disciplines enable us to explore new terrain with the confidence that God is with us every step of the way.

As we *study* the things of the spirit and the world, we become aware of our own limitations and our dependence on a power greater than ourselves. This leads to *surrender* to the God of our understanding. As we surrender we are drawn into *service,* so that we might reach out to others and in turn share God's gifts and guidance.

In order to serve with power and purpose, it is necessary for us to refresh and refuel ourselves with *silence* and to draw away from the world in solitude, where we can meet God in meditation and prayer. As we become sensitive to God's voice, we begin to see the wisdom of His word in Scripture to live *in* the world but not *of* the world. And this helps us to take our emphasis off material things and to embrace the spiritual gifts of *simplicity.*

Solvency, then, becomes the natural outflow of a simple, clutter-free life. And when a woman is free to study, surrender, and serve without hindrance, to embrace silence, simplicity, and solvency without question, she will naturally and supernaturally live in a state of *serenity.*

At times the streams may seem to disappear in the vast sea of sand around us, and we may feel our spirits go dry. But "the LORD God is a sun and shield . . . no good thing will He withhold from those who walk uprightly" (Ps. 84:11).

PART FOUR

Life on the Other Side of Debt

13

Building a Support System

As you recover from debt, one of the most important and effective gifts you can give yourself is a *support system.* I have discovered over the past ten years that I cannot live a productive and serene life without help. I believe God intended for us to draw strength from one another. The Bible tells us that when there is no guidance people fall, but there is victory for those who seek the counsel of many (see Prov. 11:14).

Now I surround myself with support on every level of my life—spiritual, physical, mental, emotional, social, and financial. Following are some suggestions, based on my experience and that of other women in recovery, that may be of help to you as you build your own support system.

Stay connected to people

The tendency of women in debt is to withdraw when we are in pain. In fact isolation is one of the key factors that got us into trouble in the first place when we attempted to solve our problems through our own strength. I urge you to reach out to others and stay connected.

Join a Twelve Step recovery program. I can think of no better way to maintain your solvency and serenity than to attend regular meetings of Debtors Anonymous or Gamblers Anonymous. These and other Twelve Step groups are based on the original Twelve Steps of Alcoholics Anonymous, which has been responsible for millions of people worldwide achieving and maintaining sobriety. Even though these groups have adapted AA's program to problems other than alcoholism and in doing so do not imply that AA either approves or endorses their adaptations or programs, DA and GA offer the same kind of opportunity for those who want to achieve and maintain solvency.

Overcomers Outreach is also patterned after AA, but is designed for Christian believers who look to Jesus Christ as their higher power. This Twelve Step group welcomes people with every kind of addiction—either process or chemical—and is committed to studying Scripture as it relates to the Twelve Steps and to praying for the needs of each individual.

Many Christians feel this group, founded by Bob and Pauline Bartosch, has done more for Christians in recovery than any other group. In a recent interview on Rich Buhler's radio program, "Table Talk," Bob said their goal is to "get a whole healing community around a hurting person."[1] To accomplish this, they recommend that individuals go for private Christian counseling in addition to attending Overcomers Outreach or another Twelve Step group.

Overcomers Outreach does not deal with money issues in the same focused way that DA and GA do. However, some people attend both groups and find this an effective way to meet their practical and spiritual needs. They work with the tools of DA or GA and receive Christ-centered support from Overcomers Outreach.

One of the most valuable tools offered in DA and GA is something called the Pressure Group, designed to help you take pressure off yourself. Typically a Pressure Group consists of you and two others, usually a man and a woman.

A meeting of the group might last one to two hours. During this time you have the opportunity to lay out your financial situation, discuss options for debt repayment, and set up a realistic spending plan, that includes money for things that bring you happiness and a sense of well-being. For one woman it might be fresh flowers; for another it might be a membership in a health club.

The idea is to make room in your spending plan for yourself

—not just for your creditors. Members of DA are committed to repaying all debts. Bankruptcy is never encouraged or endorsed. However, through bitter experience, most members have come to realize that unless they take care of themselves first they will not have the stamina or the resources to pay what they owe. The spending plan allows for both. You will also receive suggestions and guidance on how to contact your creditors to advise them of your repayment plans.

Typical meetings of Twelve Step programs last about an hour and include an opening prayer, announcements, pertinent readings, and voluntary sharing, when members of the group speak individually for three to five minutes, or longer if needed, about their struggle with money issues, their progress with their programs, and where they are in the recovery process.

It is a safe and sane environment in which to listen, share, learn, and practice the Twelve Steps of recovery, which include admitting we are powerless over our addiction, belief in a power greater than ourselves who can restore us to sanity, and making a decision to turn over our wills and our lives to God's care.

Find a support partner

A helpful facet of Twelve Step programs is sponsorship. Sponsors are people who have been in the program for six months or more and are practicing solvency one day at a time. Newcomers are encouraged to ask someone to be their sponsor. They can then turn to those people for support and guidance as they move through the Twelve Steps of the program.

Another option I have found beneficial in my life is teaming up with a friend for the purpose of mutual support. For the past ten years I have been involved in a partnership with my friend Clarissa. We talk once or twice a month, sometimes by phone, sometimes in person, depending on our schedules. We focus on our career goals and financial growth, sharing news, updating each other on previously set goals, and establishing new ones for the next time period.

Clarissa is one of the real treasures of my life. We have learned from each other, cried and laughed together, given each other wisdom and insight, and generally upheld each other as we've each carved out the career of our dreams.

My friend Dianna and I have been prayer partners for over five years. We talk and pray with each other by phone every Friday night for about twenty minutes, depending on our needs. Our personal histories are very similar, so we have become for each other a safe haven where we are listened to and loved, no matter what. The healing power of these special times cannot be measured in words. I feel totally blessed at the end of each of our sessions.

Seek advice

If I want to make a major purchase, invest a sum of money, buy an insurance policy, plan a trip, or make a business-related financial decision, I call people I have connected with in business or through my support groups and talk over the details before taking action.

Those of us with a history of denial, guilt, and grandiosity around money need the counsel of many. I find that talking through the process helps me discover where I am being unrealistic or imprudent, or wise and thoughtful. Sometimes just a question or a shared experience from the other party provides the balance I need. There is nothing like a good sounding board.

Start a journal

A few years ago when I was in deep pain over my money issues, I approached a counselor friend at the church I attend. He listened to me patiently, offered some encouragement, and then suggested that I begin keeping a journal. I was hesitant at first, but then decided to try it for a month. I've been journaling ever since.

The thing I like most about writing in a journal is that there is no one way to do it. It is as individual as each person. You can record events and expenses, share your feelings about your money issues, noting patterns of spending or shopping or gambling or whatever it is you do, write a letter to God, or create a dialogue with money itself, going back and forth. For example:

Karen: Hi, Money. I feel silly talking to an inanimate object, but someone suggested I try this in order to relieve the tension I'm feeling in my relationship with you.
Money: Good! Nice to hear from you. What's on your mind?
Karen: You are. Day and night. I can't get along with you. I can't get along without you. What's going on?
Money: Hey, don't blame me. I'm an inanimate object, remember? You're the one who calls the shots, not me. . . .

And so on. In just one five-minute writing session, I discovered that I had given money a God-like status in my life, when in fact money itself felt powerless without my direction. It was a powerful experience, and I have repeated the process on many occasions to defuse out-of-control feelings and to gain clarity. I recommend it. Just begin and see where it takes you. You can stop at any time or when you feel yourself running dry at that particular time.

Affirm your goodness and your goals

An affirmation is a positive thought or statement that you consciously repeat to produce a desired result. For example: *I, Karen, earn, manage, and share money through the power of God within me for the good of everyone concerned.*

Whether we realize it or not, many of us affirm and confirm our financial condition by the words we speak: *"I can't afford it." "I hate money; I've never understood it." "I don't have money for that right now."* These self-defeating messages actually create our reality. We have more power than we know.

Instead of affirming the negative, affirm the positive and feed your spirit messages of hope and encouragement. For example: *"Today I open myself to learning one new thing about money." "Money is my friend." "Money is coming my way as God provides for my every need."*

You may also wish to use Jesus' teaching on prosperity as the basis for your affirmations. I can't think of anything more spiritually health-giving than to feed on the Word of God.

My purpose is to give life in all its fullness. (John 10:10 TLB)

The Lord will work out His plans for my life—for your lovingkindness, Lord, continues forever. (Ps. 138:8 TLB)

"Seek first the kingdom of God and His righteousness, and all these things shall be added to you. (Matt. 6:33)

You shall remember the LORD your God, for it is He who gives you power to get wealth. (Deut. 8:18)

I like to insert my name into these passages to make them personal. Try it for yourself and see how it feels.

"My purpose is to give life to you, **Karen,** *in all its fullness."* (John 10:10)
"Karen, *you shall remember the LORD your God, for it is He who gives you power to get wealth."* (Deut. 8:18)

When I say and hear my name, I am reminded of God's will and love for me, and it helps me stay connected to Him as the true source of everything I need and want.

Pray and wait

The apostle Paul counseled the Ephesians to "put on the whole armor of God," that they would be able to "stand" firm against the evil that was all around them (see Eph. 6:11). Then he reminded them that their struggle was not against flesh and blood but against the powers and principalities of the world. How well those of us who struggle with debt know this to be true!

How often we have tried to heal ourselves through the sheer force of our own wills, by promising yet another time to stop our self-destructive spending or shopping or gambling or enabling, only to fall again. We can do battle only when we are wearing the armor of God—His shield, His helmet, His sword. Then, after having done all we can, we must stand firm, waiting on God to complete the work He started within us.

Jesus counsels us that "all things, whatever you ask in prayer, believing, you will receive" (Matt. 21:22). It is up to each of us to discover for ourselves the joy and healing that await us through prayer—our lifeline to God.

14

Sanity, Serenity, Solvency: A Way of Life

When other women tell Miki they're not sure they can relate to the spiritual side of recovery, she is quick to respond, "What other side is there?"

Miki believes that compulsions are "the result of a spiritual emptiness that drives us to behave in an insane way." For her sanity, serenity, and solvency are possible only because of her relationship with God. Through her participation in Twelve Step programs, Miki says, "I now have the knowledge and practical tools to handle my money. But only God can remove my compulsions."

Today Miki turns everything in her life over to God—her issues with under-earning and overeating, her relationships with her daughter and husband, and her work life. "Tell me what to do, and I'll do it," is her daily prayer. "I also know," she says, "that God expects me to do the footwork."

Miki attends two Twelve Step recovery programs, and she talks and prays with her sponsors each week. She has worked out a spending plan and is looking at ways to increase her income and her standard of living. "This time," she says, "I really want to do it God's way."

A PERSONAL GOD

One of the things that struck me while talking with Miki and other women, and also thinking about my own process, was the incredibly personal way God has met each one of us on our journies. Some, like Miki, have been delivered from self-will. Many, like Kelly, met God through a Twelve Step program. And others, including me, came into a relationship with Jesus Christ after our lives fell apart. But the important thing is that God makes Himself real to those who seek Him.

SPIRITUAL SNAPSHOTS

In this final chapter, I've included a few spiritual snapshots of some of the women you've met in these pages. What do they do to retain their sanity, serenity, and solvency? How do they relate to God, and how does He reveal Himself in their lives?

Some women, like Marcie, whose issue is self-debting, are still exploring their spirituality. Others, like Anne Marie, who acknowledges herself as a debting enabler, came into recovery with a spiritual foundation. She is now out of debt and making rapid progress earning, saving, and investing.

Marcie is struggling with God as her provider, because for so long there was no one to turn to but herself. Today, however, she is feeling more serene as she works through her incest issues in private therapy. "I am also working on the *idea* of a higher power," she says. "I go to spiritual retreats to help me with this. And I use the phone a lot," calling people for support whenever she has financial decisions to make or when she is feeling weak or vulnerable. Marcie, like all of the women I spoke with, attends regular meetings of various Twelve Step support programs for the sharing and support they offer.

God has softened Nancy's heart since she has embraced recovery from alcoholism and debting. "Now I take God into my work and my personal life," she says, her voice glowing with praise. She attends a spiritual service each week and continues to affirm "God will provide."

Kelly, who has struggled with pauperism, says with conviction in her voice, "Knowing God is the most astounding thing that ever happened to me. Today, I align my will with God's and hear Him gently telling me there is plenty for me." She is eager to share some of the miracles that God has worked in her life around financial and spiritual recovery. "I have always had a hard time buying myself the clothes I need," she says. "I usually wore an old T-shirt to bed, but what I really wanted was a beautiful pink nightgown. One day as my husband and I were driving I noticed something pink lying in the street. I had to stop. My husband pulled over, I jumped out of the car, and there was a pink nightie, embossed, stylish, brand-new. It still had the store tag on it. All I could say was 'Oh my God!' My breath was taken away." Kelly picked up the nightie, hopped back in the car, and thanked God. "I told Him that however He brings things into my life is great with me," she said with a lilt in her voice.

Another time Kelly needed a pair of size eleven low-heeled white pumps to go with a suit, but she didn't have the money. God delivered again. Her grandmother gave her the exact shoes she desired, without even knowing Kelly was in need. "I am such a tangible person, it's been difficult for me to believe in God," Kelly says, but she admits with a big smile that God is removing that difficulty in some pretty awesome—and tangible—ways!

Julie spends many hours a day working on her gift business. But before she begins work each morning, she spends twenty minutes in meditation and an hour walking along the beach near her home. "And then I get down on my knees," she says, "and say my daily prayers. I hear God whisper, 'I love you, Julie.' God speaks so gently. We have to pay attention or we'll miss Him."

Julie also embraces the principles of Debtors Anonymous and attends regular meetings in order to deal with her overspending. "The first time I went," she says, "I sat there with my arms tightly crossed, and I left feeling angry. I found out that I had a lot of growing up to do." Months later she returned, "and that time I felt the spirituality. I felt as if I were being welcomed home."

Suzanne, who spent most of her life being taken care of financially by others, is now experiencing being cared for by the one who really matters to her—Jesus Christ. "We're studying the book of James in the women's group I attend at church," she says. "This has helped me so much with the trials and tribulations in my life. I am also in a women's therapy group where we can talk and share our problems with one another. Two of the books we've studied that I recommend highly are *Feeling Good* and *The Feeling Good Handbook* by David Burns, M.D."

Suzanne also hosts a Debtors Anonymous meeting in the community room of the apartment building where she lives. DA has helped her come to terms with overspending and to come out of "terminal vagueness."

When Anne Marie joined Debtors Anonymous, she was grateful to find that the principles of DA are compatible with the Quaker attitudes and beliefs she practices as a member of the Society of Friends. "We believe in being quick to repay debts," she says, "in being good stewards over our possessions, and in living a peace-oriented life." Now she feels she has a good balance between the practical and the spiritual side of her recovery.

Dianne, also a Quaker, says that even though she attended church every Sunday for twenty-five years, she still "wrestled with God and was angry with Him" over her abusive marriage and unsettling divorce. "But now, in recovery, I see that God doesn't make or not make life easy for us. That depends on how we behave and what we do."

Before entering DA, however, Dianne had "compartmentalized the debting, the enabling, and the abuse. I didn't see that as part of my daily life." She used denial to hide her pain. But today, Dianne's spiritual recovery is coming about through a gradual healing with her mother, private therapy, her church support, and Debtors Anonymous.

After Toni left convent life she had a number of spiritual, emotional, and financial issues to work through. Today she attends church each Sunday. "I also meditate once or twice every day," she says, "and listen to spiritually motivating tapes, say affirmations, and pray for others."

Toni says she has an especially soft heart for people without money, because she knows firsthand the pain of that condition. She admits to still suffering from a certain amount of clutter in her life. "I believe I'm learning a major lesson about not living in chaos. I still leave dishes in the sink, piles of paper in my office, and clothes on the floor." But she no longer wants to let the condition of her finances dictate that behavior. "Now I see that true spirituality is living in peace and taking care of yourself regardless of the circumstances. Debt creates chaos, but when I look out at all that is around me, I can't say I don't have enough. It's up to me to trust God to provide."

Roberta grew up Catholic, but "Today that's not 'it' for me," she says. For a while she struggled with the oppression of her Catholic upbringing. "I had trouble with the nuns in school. Later I lived in fear of being controlled."

Now Roberta is working with a counselor who is helping her with her spiritual program and the core issues that fueled her spending and credit card abuse. She also keeps a journal and meets with other journal writers every two weeks. The Twelve Step recovery programs have helped Roberta come to terms with money issues, codependence, and fear of control.

Chris says she has had some true miracles in her life. "After completing nine of the Twelve Steps in my program for over-eaters, all of the promises the program lists—except the one about money—had come true. But now after over a year in DA, even that promise is being fulfilled. I have hardly any financial insecurity now.

Chris has also stopped debting completely. She has been solvent since she started the program, despite her problems with under-earning. "I am more conscious of asking for God's guidance," she says. "I really believe God wants me to be prosperous. And I feel prosperous now that I am living within my means and not debting."

Today Chris is pursuing work in the counseling field, in which she was trained and where she now feels called to work.

Chris is grateful for Twelve Step programs, because they have had a major part in her spiritual awakening. "I needed to apply the steps of recovery specifically to money," she says. "I was an atheist before I entered a recovery program twelve years ago. Now I am a believer. God is personal to me, and my faith is strong. I know I can communicate with God whenever I want to. This is the most important thing in my life."

Chris's recovery program includes daily prayer, dialoguing with God, talking with her sponsor, attending meetings, and serving as a sponsor and phone partner for other women in debt.

A HOPE AND A FUTURE

My own recovery is also filled with the grace of God and the fruit of much hard work. I'm happy to share that my husband and I have joined forces in our war on debt and in our commitment to God.

Charles is now in management at Nordstrom in San Diego, one of the finest clothing and shoe stores in the country. Thanks to a generous employee discount on all merchandise, our clothing needs are now fully met, and we are well-dressed. We also have a wonderful medical plan that allows us to meet our health needs.

As of June of this year, I am completely debt-free, and for the first time in years I have a savings account, a growing retirement plan, and a fund for taxes and investments. My husband's goal is to be debt-free by the end of the year. We live a completely solvent lifestyle now, paying cash for everything.

Together we have embraced the discipline of simplicity and have a more prosperous and peaceful life than ever before. We have come to treasure our cozy Saturday night dates at home with a rented video and a homemade vegetarian pizza (my specialty).

I listen to classical music on the radio now instead of purchasing expensive symphony tickets. We take long walks on the beach and hike in the mountains instead of going to resorts or hotels.

We pray each morning, turning our wills and our lives, our families, our finances, and our workplaces over to God. We tithe, and God multiplies that money and brings it back to us. I have almost eliminated worry from my life. I am able to see the lesson behind the problems and pain now in a way I couldn't years ago.

Money has also come into our lives in some wondrous ways: promotions for my husband, gifts, pay increases, new writing opportunities, surprises such as equity in an insurance policy, free airline tickets from accumulated "advantage mileage" I had forgotten about, speaking engagements, teaching weekends, and through selling books, record albums, and other possessions we no longer need or want.

This week we received word that our request for refurbishing our apartment has been granted. We will receive a brand-new dishwasher, stove, and refrigerator, new kitchen flooring, and refinished cabinets, as well as new paint throughout.

And while I was writing this chapter, the first of two brand-new free pairs of shoes worth over $200 each arrived from the manufacturer. Both are gifts from my husband, the result of a sales contest he won at work. I am convinced now that our most basic needs, as well as our most ardent wishes, are as dear to God as we are.

We have joined the Kenneth Copeland Ministries' spiritual "War on Debt" and follow their daily television broadcasts. We attended Ron Blue's "Master Your Money" video and study series at our church for more spiritual and practical help with finances. And we surround ourselves with support, through the prayer chain at our church, Twelve Step groups, and private counseling. These are just some of the financial blessings we've received—blessings that are available to you too as you align with God's will for your life.

My prayer, as you recover from overspending, compulsive shopping, credit card abuse, gambling, enabling, under-earning, self-debting, or pauperism, is that you will keep your eyes on God, trusting the promise He gave us through the prophet Jeremiah nearly three thousand years ago. " 'For I know the plans I have for you,' declares the LORD, 'plans to prosper you and not to harm you, plans to give you hope and a future' " (Jer. 29:11 NIV).

SUPPLEMENTARY RESOURCES

Books

Celebration of Discipline: The Path to Spiritual Growth, by Richard Foster. Harper & Row, 1988. An inspiring and practical book on the classical spiritual disciplines for anyone who wishes to break free of superficial habits and draw closer to God.

Do What You Love, the Money Will Follow, by Marsha Sinetar. Dell, 1989. An inspiring and practical guide to making a living by expressing your talents and passions.

Facing Codependence, by Pia Mellody et al. Harper & Row, 1989. A definitive guide to understanding the origins of codependence and the path to recovery by a nationally known authority on codependence.

How to Be a Financially Secure Woman, by Mary Elizabeth Schlayer, with Marilyn H. Cooley. Ballantine, 1987. An expert's guide for the woman who wants financial savvy and independence.

How to Get Out of Debt, Stay Out of Debt, and Live Prosperously (based on the proven principles and techniques of Debtors Anonymous), by Jerrold Mundis. Bantam, 1988. A simple, effective formula for freeing yourself from debt and staying that way.

Journey Notes: Writing for Recovery and Spiritual Growth, by Richard Solley and Roseann Lloyd. Harper & Row, 1989. This practical and helpful guide is for anyone who uses writing for self-discovery and personal growth, as well as those who keep journals in Twelve Step programs.

Master Your Money: A Step-by-Step Plan for Financial Freedom, by Ron Blue. Thomas Nelson Publishers, 1991. The author, a recognized financial advisor, combines the wisdom of the Bible on stewardship with up-to-date advice on financial management.

Pain and Pretending, expanded edition with Study Guide, by Rich Buhler. Thomas Nelson Publishers, 1991. A significant resource on the pain and recovery of victimization by a seasoned counselor, minister, talk-show host, and expert on the topic.

A Woman's Guide to Financial Peace of Mind, by Ron and Judy Blue. Focus on the Family Books, 1991. Practical and inspiring help for women on all facets of finance, based on Ron Blue's career as a financial counselor and the authors' experience raising two sons and three daughters.

Women Who Shop Too Much: Overcoming the Urge to Splurge, by Carolyn Wesson. St. Martin's Press, 1990. Informative self-help guide focusing on problem shopping and spending, as well as in-depth steps to recovery for compulsive shoppers.

Organizations and support groups

Consumer Credit Counseling Service

A nonprofit organization that provides budget, credit, and debt counseling *free* of charge. This is not a collection or lending institution. The service helps people help themselves to solve their debt problems. For information about offices in your area or elsewhere in the United States, call their toll-free number: 800/388-2226.

Debtors Anonymous General Service Board
P.O. Box 20322
New York, NY 10025-9992
Telephone: 212/642-8222

For information about meetings in your area, see the listing in your local telephone book or write to the address above, providing a stamped, self-addressed envelope. All requests are kept confidential. Since this office is run by volunteers, however, response time may be slow.

Gamblers Anonymous International Service Office
P.O. Box 17173
Los Angeles, CA 90017
Telephone: 213/386-8789

For information about meetings in your area, see the listing in your local telephone book or write to the address above, providing a stamped, self-addressed envelope. All requests are kept confidential. Since this office is run by volunteers, however, response time may be slow.

Kenneth Copeland Ministries
Fort Worth, TX 76192

Write for information about materials and program listings pertaining to their "War On Debt" series.

National Foundation For Consumer Credit
8701 Georgia Ave., Suite 507
Silver Spring, MD 20910
Telephone: 800/388-2227

This nonprofit organization offers help with debt and has associated offices throughout the United States.

Overcomers Outreach
2290 W. Whittier Blvd., Suite A
La Habra, CA 90631

Send a donation of $11.00 to cover postage and materials, which include literature describing the program and a format for establishing the Outreach in your church or area.

Shopaholics, Limited
15 W. 18th St.
New York, NY 10011
Telephone: 212/675-4342

Offers support groups and workshops for compulsive spenders in the New York metropolitan area. Provides information nationwide. If you live outside the New York area, send a stamped, self-addressed envelope with your request for materials.

South Oaks Hospital Gambler's National Help Line
800/732-9808

NOTES

CHAPTER 2

1. From "Prosperity, Success and Codependence" seminar by Sondra Mehlhop, Ph.D., and an in-person interview in June 1991. Used by permission.
2. From interviews and discussions on "Talk From The Heart" radio program series 1989-90.
3. Pia Mellody, *Facing Codependence* (San Francisco, CA: Harper & Row, 1989), 4.
4. All subsequent quotations by Mehlhop are excerpted from an interview in June 1991 and are used by permission.

CHAPTER 3

1. From an in-person interview, July 1991. Used by permission.

CHAPTER 4

1. Daniel Goleman, "Reigning In a Compulsion to Spend," *The New York Times,* July 17, 1991, B8.

CHAPTER 6

1. Earl Ubell, "Are You A Gambler?" *Parade Magazine,* June 8, 1991, 8.
2. From a telephone conversation with Dr. Blume, August 1991, and from her published material, "Gambling Problems in Alcoholics and Drug Addicts," chapter 53 in *Comprehensive Handbook of Drug and Alcohol Addiction,* edited by Norman S. Miller (New York: Marcel Dekker, 1991), 967-974. Used by permission.
3. From a telephone interview with Dr. Lesieur, July 1991. Used by permission.
4. Gwenda Blair, "Betting Against the Odds," *The New York Times Magazine,* September 25, 1988, 76.
5. Tomas M. Martinez, *The Gambling Scene* (Springfield, IL: Charles C. Thomas, 1983), cited in "The Psychology of Gam-

bling," by Igor Kusyszyn, *The Annals of the American Academy,* July 1984, 137.

CHAPTER 7

1. From radio program "Talk From The Heart," 1990.
2. Robin Norwood, *Women Who Love Too Much,* (New York: Pocket Books, 1985).
3. Norwood, 221.

CHAPTER 8

1. From an in-person interview, June 1991. Used by permission.
2. From an in-person interview, June 1991. Used by permission.

CHAPTER 9

1. Rich Buhler, *Pain and Pretending* (Nashville, TN: Thomas Nelson Publishers, 1988), 137.

CHAPTER 11

1. Susan Jacoby, "Compulsive Shopping," *Glamour,* 1986, 350.

CHAPTER 12

1. Richard Foster, *Celebration of Discipline* (San Francisco, CA: Harper & Row, 1978), 30.
2. *Alcoholics Anonymous* (New York: Alcoholics Anonymous World Services, Inc., 1976), 59.
3. An old Shaker hymn. Author unknown.
4. Foster, 74.
5. Paraphrase of a prayer composed by Reinhold Niebuhr, cited in *Bartlett's Familiar Quotations* by John Bartlett (Boston,

MA: Little, Brown, 1968), 1024. This paraphrase is often used in Twelve Step programs.

CHAPTER 13

1. Interview on "Table Talk," June 26, 1991.

About the Author

Karen O'Connor has had firsthand experience with self-debting and debting enabling and began her recovery more than three years ago. She writes this book, *When Spending Takes the Place of Feeling,* as her testimony to the healing she has experienced through a spiritual program of surrender and dependence on God.

She is an award-winning author of more than thirty books, hundreds of magazine articles, and two educational films. She is an experienced teacher, speaker, and seminar leader and has led workshops and classes for a variety of businesses, women's groups, and schools throughout the country. Currently she teaches writing classes and seminars through the University of California Extension School and the Institute of Children's Literature.

The mother of three adult children, she lives in San Diego with her husband, Charles Flowers.